W9-CLH-814

"We all experience loneliness. In this book Ruth Graham, drawing on her own experiences and biblical narrative, shows how God can transform our loneliness into a positive experience that draws us into a closer, more meaningful relationship with Him."

Mark Batterson, *New York Times* bestselling author
of *The Circle Maker*; lead pastor of National
Community Church

"This book is a perfect, timely, beautiful gift. Many of us experience loneliness yet struggle to be able to say that out loud. I know I have. Ruth gives words to our pain and comfort to our souls and helps us see that our God who transforms everything offered to Him can transform our loneliness too."

Sheila Walsh, cohost of *Life Today*; author of *Holding On
When You Want To Let Go*

"*Loneliness* is a word that often causes us to wince or change the subject. It can be a highly painful and empty experience of the heart, and research shows that today it is far more common than we have ever known. However, Ruth Graham's book provides a fresh and helpful biblical lens on the concept, which is that loneliness can actually be a path to something much greater, and more purposeful, than we ever imagined. Her deeply vulnerable stories, scriptural principles, and practical steps will change you forever. Highly recommended."

John Townsend, PhD, *New York Times* bestselling author
of *Boundaries*; founder of the Townsend Institute
for Leadership and Counseling

"To any of us—and indeed, all of us—who have experienced lonely times, I am delighted to recommend Ruth Graham's latest book. In it she invites us to cooperate with God as He transforms our loneliness into something that meets our needs and brings Him glory."

Dr. Eric L. Motley, author of *Madison Park: A Place of Hope*; executive vice president of the Aspen Institute, Washington, DC

"My dear friend Ruth Graham has written a timely book that sheds light on the continuously growing issue of loneliness, which at some point will be a struggle for every person. Ruth courageously shares her personal battle with loneliness and offers valuable insight on how we can work with God instead of against Him in our loneliest times. Get ready to experience how God can purpose loneliness for His Kingdom plans!"

Dr. Benny Tate Sr., pastor of Rock Springs Church, Milner, GA

Transforming Loneliness

DEEPENING OUR RELATIONSHIPS
WITH **GOD** AND **OTHERS**
WHEN WE FEEL ALONE

Ruth Graham
WITH **CINDY LAMBERT**

BakerBooks
a division of Baker Publishing Group
Grand Rapids, Michigan

© 2021 by Ruth Graham

Published by Baker Books
a division of Baker Publishing Group
PO Box 6287, Grand Rapids, MI 49516-6287
www.bakerbooks.com

Printed in the United States of America

All rights reserved. No part of this publication may be reproduced, stored in a retrieval system, or transmitted in any form or by any means—for example, electronic, photocopy, recording—without the prior written permission of the publisher. The only exception is brief quotations in printed reviews.

Library of Congress Cataloging-in-Publication Data
Names: Graham, Ruth, 1950– author. | Lambert, Cindy, author.
Title: Transforming loneliness : deepening our relationships with God and others
    when we feel alone / Ruth Graham and Cindy Lambert.
Description: Grand Rapids, Michigan : Baker Books, a division of Baker Publishing
    Group, [2021] | Includes bibliographical references.
Identifiers: LCCN 2021003782 | ISBN 9780801094279 (cloth) | ISBN 9781540901583
    (paperback) | ISBN 9781493432851 (ebook)
Subjects: LCSH: Loneliness—Religious aspects—Christianity. | Spiritual
    life—Christianity. | Spirituality—Christianity. | Silence—Religious aspects—
    Christianity. | Solitude—Religious aspects—Christianity.
Classification: LCC BV4911.G73 2021 | DDC 248.8/6—dc23
LC record available at https://lccn.loc.gov/2021003782

Unless otherwise indicated, Scripture quotations are from the (NASB®) New American Standard Bible®, Copyright © 1960, 1971, 1977, 1995 by The Lockman Foundation. Used by permission. All rights reserved. www.lockman.org

Scripture quotations labeled NIV are from THE HOLY BIBLE, NEW INTERNATIONAL VERSION®, NIV® Copyright © 1973, 1978, 1984, 2011 by Biblica, Inc.® Used by permission. All rights reserved worldwide.

Scripture quotations labeled NKJV are from the New King James Version®. Copyright © 1982 by Thomas Nelson. Used by permission. All rights reserved.

Scripture quotations labeled NLT are from the Holy Bible, New Living Translation, copyright © 1996, 2004, 2007, 2013, 2015 by Tyndale House Foundation. Used by permission of Tyndale House Publishers, Inc., Carol Stream, Illinois 60188. All rights reserved.

The author is represented by Ambassador Literary Agency, Nashville, Tennessee.

Some names and identifying details have been changed to protect the privacy of individuals.

21 22 23 24 25 26 27   7 6 5 4 3 2 1

In keeping with biblical principles of creation stewardship, Baker Publishing Group advocates the responsible use of our natural resources. As a member of the Green Press Initiative, our company uses recycled paper when possible. The text paper of this book is composed in part of post-consumer waste.

green
press
INITIATIVE

For you

Contents

Loneliness is a wilderness, but through receiving it as a gift, accepting it from the hand of God, and offering it back to Him with thanksgiving, it may become a pathway to holiness, to glory, and to God Himself.

Elisabeth Elliot

The Pelican in the Wilderness

> Loneliness . . . comes mostly when we are disconnected from others in such a way that we feel ignored, overlooked, or not known as we really are. It is the painful ache in our hearts for intimate connection, belonging, and companionship.
>
> Trevor Hudson[1]

I woke to the familiar sounds of the hospital—distant beeping, footsteps in the hallway, muffled voices from the nearby nurses' station, and the constant white noise I could never quite identify. I opened my eyes to the same scene I'd been staring at for five days—white ceiling tiles covered with little black holes too numerous to count. My back ached and I longed to roll over onto my side but knew I could not. The doctor had told me to stay flat on my back, and I wasn't about to risk another wave of nausea or the sharp pains of another severe headache. I longed for some water to wet my lips. I could see the cup of water on the bed table next to me, but it was out of my reach without sitting up and I dared not. *I just need to wait for the nurse*, I thought. *It shouldn't be long.* But the minutes passed slowly.

I was all alone.

Of course, I knew God was present with me. He always is. But the simple reality was that I longed for the physical presence of a caring person—someone to hold my cup so I could take a few satisfying swallows. Someone to pull my blanket a bit higher and pat my arm or squeeze my hand and remind me that my condition was just temporary—that the doctors would figure out the source of my problem and set me on the path of recovery.

A sad longing crept over me.

It wasn't just that I was alone. I was used to being alone. I'd been single for years and was used to the silence and fending for myself that comes with living in a single-person household. No, the longing I felt went beyond that of simply being *alone*. I was *lonely*. And loneliness is a feeling that goes far deeper than missing the presence of another person. It is an ache, a deep longing to feel connected, validated, seen, known, and valued. The longing I was feeling, I realized at that moment, wasn't going to be satisfied by the nurse who would soon offer me fresh water, straighten my sheets, and give me the medicine that would relieve the growing, throbbing pain in my head. My loneliness wouldn't be satisfied until Noelle and Windsor, my two daughters, walked into my room and I saw their smiling, loving faces even as they teased me, and until one of them handed me the phone and I heard the steady "I'm here, Mom," from Graham, my son. That deep connection to my children—that experience of being cared for and valued—would help chase away the sad loneliness that had been brewing not only for the past five days in the hospital but for many months before I'd been admitted.

For years I'd had back pain but no clue as to the cause. Then I began to walk like I was drunk, lose my balance, and even fall. Embarrassing and dangerous. I went to chiropractors, orthopedists, psychiatrists, and neurologists. I was told it may be Parkinson's. Since my father had Parkinson's, that concerned me, but a neurologist could not see anything wrong. Though relieved my symptoms didn't seem to be due to Parkinson's, I was very frustrated and discouraged. Finally, another neurologist did an MRI and discovered I had a tumor growing in my spinal column. It had to come out.

I was thankful to finally have the reason for my pain identified, though I was apprehensive about surgery. I asked for the best neurosurgeon around and found a wonderful doctor at Virginia Commonwealth University, about two hours from my home. All three children came to see me off. Noelle lived near me, but Graham and Windsor lived many hours away. We had a big family dinner the night before, and the next morning my two daughters drove me to Richmond while my son stayed back to do some needed chores at my home.

It was a four-hour surgery and all went well. Afterward, the girls went home to their families. I was alone and in pain but well taken care of by the staff at the hospital. I was there for four days, then went home. The girls argued their best to have someone come take care of me, but I am stubborn and independent and did not want that. I'd tried my best before the surgery to put up meals and arrange my kitchen so that I would not have to bend, lift, or twist. A home healthcare nurse came each day to check on me, as well as physical therapists. I progressed, but between the pain and fatigue, I did not feel well.

About a month later, I observed a small swelling at the base of my incision. It grew to the size of an egg. My eldest daughter, Noelle, who is a nurse, took a look at it and didn't like it. I called the doctor the next day. They asked me to send a picture to them, which I did, and they told me to lay flat for three days and then call them back. Nothing changed. They told me to stay on my back another two days. Still nothing changed. By this time, I was unable to keep food down and had a constant, pounding headache. I asked Windsor to come take care of me.

The doctors determined I had developed a spinal fluid leak. Finally, I was told they'd have to put in a lumbar drain at the hospital. I wasn't at all sure I could make the two-hour trip. But the next morning the girls drove me back to Richmond. I lay on the back seat with a bucket on the floor, just in case.

Five days later I was staring at ceiling tiles, waiting for the nurse to bring me fresh ice water. My condition still hadn't changed. I was very discouraged. Because my girls lived hours away from the hospital, they couldn't visit regularly. I'd been unable to read because of the headaches. So I'd watched endless news about the upcoming election and, of course, I'd prayed. I'd been so lonely.

Late that morning, the doctors came into my room and told me the surgery would have to be redone. The dura around my spinal column was fragile to begin with, due to my age, and apparently the stitching had not been able to hold. They would restitch and glue the dura for a stronger hold. The next morning I'd be back in surgery. My children could not leave their homes and jobs on such short notice, so I was alone to face this surgery. They would await a phone call telling them all was well.

As I lay in bed that afternoon, waiting for the next day's surgery, I thought a lot about loneliness. In my lifetime I'd waged some serious battles with it. I had the emotional scars to remind me how hard those battles had been. And by this point in my life I knew enough about loneliness to know that it is a formidable foe—one to be taken seriously. One that requires an intentional battle plan and strong weapons to fight lest that loneliness take root in my soul and grow, spilling over into my overall well-being.

For loneliness, unchallenged, has the power to eat away at our emotional, spiritual, and physical health. It was time to get serious about addressing this challenge, because I knew that after my surgery, I had a long and painful recovery ahead of me, and I'd be facing most of that time at home alone. *Could I manage*, I wondered, *to be alone but not be lonely?*

How blessed I was that the next day the surgery was performed and I could begin the healing process. The children were relieved, and I was soon home. Home alone and serious about working with God on my loneliness. As it turned out, my recovery was long and slow, so I had lots of time to work on it!

The Birth of a Book

The last thing on my mind at the time was writing a book on loneliness. I just wanted to make it through my recovery without succumbing to self-pity and depression. I wanted my faith to grow through the ordeal. I wanted the suffering to count for something. I wanted to emerge from my recovery stronger than I had been going into it. As I look back now, I believe that's when God started writing this book in my heart. Though He didn't let me in on that fact for a few years, I can't say I'm surprised to realize it now.

Each book God has led me to write had its birth in painful experience. After all, isn't that where God grows and stretches us? It is for me!

I didn't write this book because I am an expert on "curing" or "overcoming" loneliness. I don't write books from academic expertise. I write them from my personal struggles—my exploration into Scripture and my questions of others who've gone before me or suffered with me. It's through my research and reading that I find God sheds His light into my dark places. I wrote *In Every Pew Sits a Broken Heart* because I'd been broken and was finding God's light in the journey. I wrote *Fear Not Tomorrow, God Is Already There* because my struggle with fear was leading me to experience God's presence in the face of fear. I wrote *Forgiving My Father, Forgiving Myself* because God's forgiveness was infiltrating my lack of forgiveness. And now I invite you to join me on my journey through loneliness.

All too often we are so ashamed of the battles we face that we fail to share honestly with one another the work God is doing in our lives. But I believe something beautiful and supernatural occurs when believers are honest and transparent with one another about our struggles and discoveries as we live out our faith walk and experience God's intervention in our lives. This is why the body of Christ is so crucially important to our spiritual growth. When we see God at work in the struggles of other believers—both those whose stories are told in Scripture and those who walk the earth with us now—our faith in God's power to intervene in our own lives grows stronger.

So welcome, not only to my ups and downs with loneliness but to God's work in the loneliness in my life and in the lives of many others. From Jonah in the belly of the fish, to some current military spouses whose loved ones are serving in harm's way, to the apostle John living in exile on Patmos, to some prisoners I know who are serving life sentences, to Zacchaeus the unpopular curious onlooker, to some friends I've made along the way on this journey, even to the twenty thousand people who participated in a massive Cigna survey of the experience of loneliness, we'll be exploring the whats and whys of loneliness and, more importantly, how to work with God in dealing with it in a positive way. Each step along this journey, we'll discover God at work, ready to transform our loneliness into a positive experience that accomplishes His purposes and draws us into the very thing we long for: a closer, deeper, more satisfying relationship with Him and others.

I hope you'll bring your own experiences—the good, the bad, the ugly, and the beautiful—to reading this book and even to sharing with others what you discover in these pages. Some of you will pull back at the thought of sharing your discoveries with others. Why be so vulnerable and open? Because loneliness is far more prevalent than you'd ever guess.

Vivek Murthy, surgeon general of the United States from 2014 to 2017 and cochair of President Biden's COVID-19 Advisory Board, makes an astounding claim:

> Loneliness is a growing health epidemic. We live in the most technologically connected age in the history of civilization, yet rates of loneliness have doubled since the 1980s. Today, over 40% of adults in America report feeling lonely, and research suggests that the real number may well be higher.

Additionally, the number of people who report having a close confidante in their lives has been declining over the past few decades.[2]

Over 40 percent? That's far more pervasive than I was expecting. You and I are by no means alone in our struggle. Murthy goes on to write about what will happen if we don't address this massive loneliness.

> If we cannot rebuild strong, authentic social connections, we will continue to splinter apart—in the workplace and in society. ... We must take action now to build the connections that are the foundation of strong companies and strong communities—and that ensure greater health and well-being for all of us.[3]

He makes the situation sound urgent, doesn't he? After my research for this book, I, too, believe that addressing our loneliness is critical.

The bout of loneliness I described above wasn't my first, nor would it be my last. In fact, as I write these words, I'm certain I will battle with it again. I imagine that you will, too, for loneliness is a universal human experience. In these pages we're going to explore just how universal it is, why it is so important to address, and how we can experience true transformation of our loneliness.

You probably bought this book because you know the longing to be known, seen, touched, heard, and understood; to be wanted, enjoyed, and needed; to be valued and validated. You and I and the rest of the human family want to know we matter to someone, and we long for the sense of belonging that comes from true companionship.

Shattering the Power of Shame

Until I began working on this book, I wasn't aware how common and how easy it is to feel ashamed for being lonely, but it turns out many of us find it embarrassing to admit we struggle with loneliness.

My first clue came one day while flying to a speaking engagement. Since I was working on this book, I'd been reading quite a few books on loneliness, and I'd taken one along to read on the plane. But as I began to pull it out of my bag I suddenly stopped. Did I really want the man sitting next to me to think I was lonely? No, I didn't. I let the book slide unnoticed back into my bag. Another day I did the same at a doctor's office. Why?

Could it be that we fear being lonely means we are somehow deficient? That we don't want to be found out for being lacking or inadequate—either because we don't have more close friends or because we are unable to enjoy solitude? If we are honest with ourselves, it's embarrassing. Is it just me, or do you, too, squirm at the thought of being found out as a lonely person?

Well, we can both stop squirming. It's not just us. In *The Lonely American*, Professor Jacqueline Olds explains that many patients seeking help for anxiety or depression don't want to admit when their problem is also loneliness. "We found it was very difficult for our patients to talk about their isolation, which seemed to fill them with deep shame. We noticed they were far more comfortable saying they were depressed than lonely."⁴ So what do we do? We cover our pain. We mask it. We keep it secret. And by doing so, we increase our sense of isolation—of not being truly known. "Even in laughter the heart may be in pain," says Proverbs 14:13. How true. All too often the lonely suffer in silence, which heightens our feelings that no one else really understands what we think or how we feel.

I read in *Psychology Today*,

> Loneliness has a clear stigma: We tend to be able to spot and identify the lonely people around us. One study found that over a six-month period, lonely people were pushed to the periphery of social networks and surprisingly, so were their friends. Being pushed out "into the cold" in this way has a surprising effect on our bodies. . . . Loneliness actually makes us feel colder. Studies found that recalling a time in which we felt lonely made participants estimate the room temperature as being significantly colder. It even made their actual skin temperature drop.[5]

Wow! That sure gives new meaning to the phrases being "pushed out into the cold" and being "given the cold shoulder." No wonder we feel the urge to hide our loneliness! Yet the more we hide our loneliness, the more we isolate ourselves and the lonelier we become. It's a vicious cycle.

Let's face the fact right now that if you and I are going to address our loneliness and seek wisdom in dealing with it, it's going to take courage. And I mean that literally, because the fear and shame of loneliness are quite real. One census in the United Kingdom found that "loneliness is the number one fear of young people today—ranking ahead of losing a home or a job. Fully 42% of Millennial women are more afraid of loneliness than a cancer diagnosis."[6] Clearly, I'm no Millennial, but I can now look back at myself "hiding" that I was reading a book on loneliness from total strangers on an airplane and in a doctor's office, and I see that both fear and shame were at work in me. But I know from God's Word that fear and shame have no legitimate place in the life of a believer. First John 4:18 assures us, "There is no fear in love; but perfect love casts out fear," and as it says in Isaiah 54:4, "Fear not, for you will not be put to shame; and do not feel humiliated, for you will not be disgraced."

So let's begin our journey by seeking relief from the fear and shame of loneliness. There's no better place to discover the healthiest possible response to loneliness than the Word of God. I'd never before searched the Scriptures for God's perspective on loneliness, but as always, God's Word never disappoints. What a joy it was for me in the writing of this book to pore over His Word for lessons in loneliness. There God has not only gifted us with many reassuring words of empathy, comfort, and insight but has also provided us with rich, fascinating examples of His people who dealt with loneliness as they sought Him, served Him, and even fled from or followed Him.

I'm eager for you to dive into His Word with me in every chapter of this book. And I believe that Psalm 68:6 offers the perfect image to set the tone for understanding God's heart toward the lonely. It says, "God makes a home for the lonely." A *home.* The ultimate place to find deep, intimate connection and belonging—the very things the lonely heart most longs to have. Let's begin by gathering our loneliness and shame and taking them home to our Father, who will overwhelm our shame with His perfect love and satisfy our deepest longings for belonging. That is as simple as reaching out to God and expressing to Him this simple truth: *Lord,*

I am lonely. My loneliness hurts. I want the hurt to stop. I want the loneliness to end. I'm not sure where we go from here, but I'm turning to You for help and wisdom and asking You to satisfy my deepest longings for connection and belonging. Amen.

The Pelican

King David, knowing God's love and compassion, often cried out to God about his many thoughts and emotions by writing psalms. Because of this, we know that at times David, too, experienced heart-wrenching loneliness. I've listed for you in appendix C some of David's loneliness psalms, along with many other Scriptures that I find helpful when struggling with loneliness. Sometimes such verses help me express thoughts and feelings that are difficult to put into words. I hope you'll turn to this resource during and after reading this book whenever you long to ease your loneliness "at home" in God's presence.

While I was studying for this book, one of David's verses really leaped off the page for me, perhaps because the imagery he used struck me as so peculiar. Psalm 102:6–7 says, "I resemble a pelican of the wilderness; I have become like an owl of the waste places. I lie awake, I have become like a lonely bird on a housetop."

A pelican? Why a pelican? And what on earth would a pelican be doing out in the wilderness?

Anyone who knows me knows I love the beach! My children and their spouses and my grandchildren also love it. We go as a family each year and look forward to the time— laughing, teasing, talking, praying, wading and swimming, building sandcastles, and eating seafood. We anticipate it all year long.

When I am at the beach, it is my habit to rise early each morning to walk the shoreline. I like to see the sun rise over the water. As I walk, I talk to God—it seems easier to talk with Him at the beach. Maybe because there are so few distractions. But mainly I think it is because there I am surrounded by so many things that point to His glory.

The ocean is powerful. It is at times so wild that the surf roars as it tumbles and splashes, yet at other times so calm and peaceful it is as still as glass. Its depths are unfathomable, its horizon vast and endless. It is mysterious, teeming with spectacular life. It can calm and relax yet also be dangerous. It is mighty. Its tide is steady and consistent and faithful; the waves roll in hour after hour, day after day, month after month. Even when I am long gone home, it still faithfully pounds the beach.

The ocean also inspires me to awe. I love to meditate on the ways it reflects God's character. Then I spend time praising the Lord using my ABC list: *almighty, bountiful, compassionate, deliverer, enough* . . . all the way to XYZ. X: He is a *xenophile*, a friend of strangers. Y: all the "promises of God are *yes* and amen." Z: He is the *zenith* of it all, and He is *zealous* for me. I love doing that in praise to the One who created all the beauty around me as I walk.

Jesus spent a lot of time on the beach of the Sea of Galilee, so He must have enjoyed it as well. He walked by the sea after His temptation by Satan in the wilderness. Was He trying to clear His head after such an intense time with the evil one? Was He just wanting to relax and talk with His Father about His ministry that was just beginning? It was while He was walking the beach that He saw Peter and Andrew casting their nets for fish and called them to follow Him. They left their nets and followed Him. Soon He saw James and John in the boat with their father, Zebedee, and He called them to follow Him. They did as well.

Choosing these men wasn't happenstance. He didn't just bump into them. He knew before the foundation of the world that He would walk on the beach that day and call those specific men to join Him. These were men of the sea. Fishing was their livelihood. Many events took place by the sea or on it throughout Jesus's time on earth. It was a special place for Him and His disciples. After His resurrection He even cooked them fish over a fire on the beach.

For all these reasons, I feel close to the Lord whenever I'm at the beach. There, I love to observe the birds. The sandpipers run so rapidly to get the sand clams that their skinny legs are a blur. And the seagulls with their noisy calls. We quit feeding them bread because all the seagulls in the area would show up and bring their cousins. It was actually frightening the younger children! But they are fun to watch as they dip and dive with the air currents, or march across the sand calling to each other.

Every afternoon at about five o'clock, always flying in formation, come the pelicans. They are social and gregarious birds. They feed mainly on fish and rarely venture farther than twenty miles from the shore. Though sometimes a hurricane can blow them inland, they stick pretty close to the water or marshy areas. On land they look a bit gangly and awkward, but they are a beautiful sight as they glide smoothly over the water with their impressive wingspan of six to seven feet. I love to watch them spy their prey, take a deep dive beak first, capture their fish, and scoop them from the water. I never cease to be amazed at God's masterful design of their large throat pouch for catching prey and draining water.

And this is the bird that David chose as the metaphor for his psalm—a pelican. But not in its habitat, surrounded by its squadron as it should be. Not where it could draw its nourishment from the sea as it needs to. No. He paints a desperately lonely picture! Pelicans *need* the water, not the wilderness. The wilderness is no place for them. David's lonely pelican is desolate, dejected, discouraged, defeated, despairing, distressed . . . you get the picture. Is that how you feel in your loneliness?

I have experienced those very emotions at the beach. Some years ago, my then husband and I were visiting the beach after my eldest daughter's wedding. We needed the rest! But on our first day there we had an argument, and my husband became very angry with me. I tried to resolve the conflict but to no avail. He began to withdraw from me emotionally. At one point, he quit talking to me altogether. He loved the beach as much as I did, and I was sad that his emotional state was spoiling the time for both of us. We'd come there to spend the time of rest together. Instead we were both lonely. Our marriage was already in distress, and this was further evidence of it. I ached with loneliness.

I would walk the beach early as was my custom, then come back to the screened porch that overlooked a little creek and have my devotional time. I still have the many notations in my Bible from that time: Psalm 17:3, "I have purposed that my mouth will not transgress." Psalm 31:7, "I will rejoice and be glad in Your lovingkindness, because You have seen my affliction." Psalm 62:5, "My soul, wait in silence for God only, for my hope is from Him."

I prayed and begged God to help me. I bent over backward to make my husband happy and encourage him to open up. But he was shut tighter than a clam shell. I prayed and asked God to help my marriage. I was assured by Psalm 68:6, "God makes a home for the lonely." There was a place for me. I was not shut out. God was my refuge and strength and was using that time to prove that to me.

I look now at the pelican verse and see that King David seemed to know how I felt, as if we were kindred spirits. He knew loneliness from the inside out. That week at the beach seemed blown, but I did grow in my understanding of God. And I crawled into His Word to learn of Him. It's as if the loneliness I felt drove me to Jesus and His Word, where I found comfort and solace.

That's what I want for you to find as well. Comfort and solace, yet also so much more. I believe (and research confirms) that loneliness ebbs and flows over the years as our circumstances change. I don't want to be defeated by it. I don't want to succumb to it. I don't want to be ashamed of it. I don't just want to endure it. I want to know how to work *with* God and not against Him when loneliness strikes. I want to experience His power in dealing with it. I want to be awed by God's presence and power as He transforms my loneliness into a greater closeness with Him and with others. He *can* do that! He *will* do that! But experience has taught me that in order for that to happen I have to intentionally work with Him. I have a part to play. You do too.

Together, through biblical principles and examples, through eye-opening research, through true-life stories and inspiring living examples, we are going to discover how the core needs that drive our loneliness—to be seen, to be validated, to be known, to belong, and to be loved—can be met as God transforms our loneliness into a positive experience that accomplishes His purposes and draws us into a closer, more intimate, and more meaningful relationship with Him and others.

God makes a home for the lonely.

Psalm 68:6

2

The One Who Sees

The solution for loneliness is love. Specifically, the love of a
good God who sees you, sympathizes with you and possesses
the power to do something about your loneliness.

Annie Lent[1]

As I started to think about writing this book, I recognized
that so many people in my world were lonely. I could see
them in my church sitting by themselves, or pushing a cart
at my local grocery store, or sitting alone in a doctor's office.
I could see them as well in my little neighborhood that has
several widows and divorcées (like me). The neighbor ladies,
some married, some not, gathered for lunch about once a
month not only to be neighborly but to provide companionship, so I joined them when I could.

I began to watch for signs of loneliness. I have a friend who
regularly tells me he is lonely. He has no children, his siblings
are older and aging, and many of his friends are dying. He
often comes by just to read the newspaper in my sunroom,
happy to be in the company of another person. It used to

be that he'd ask me if I ever got lonely or felt loneliness. I always said no. I had my work and my children and grandchildren to keep me occupied. Though I've had a number of seasons of deep and painful loneliness, I didn't generally feel lonely. Alone, yes, but not lonely. There is such a difference. But somewhere along the line, slowly, imperceptibly at first, a growing sense of disquiet began to creep in. This isn't a book about singleness at all (as married people can suffer with loneliness just as much as singles), but in my case, I began to take notice of couples walking hand in hand or a person accompanying another to the doctor's office. I began to see couples in church, at the grocery store, at the movies, out to dinner. Even the doves in my yard were a pair!

One Valentine's Day, two of my dear friends and their husbands went to a Valentine's dinner at a local church. I felt left out. Did no one think to include me? I wouldn't have minded going as a single to a Valentine's dinner with friends at church. Was it a "couples only" event? On that Sunday morning, the pastor preached an excellent sermon on marriage. I agreed with everything he said. But I felt like the odd man out. I wasn't, of course. There were other singles there who, perhaps, were feeling the same way I was.

Quite honestly, I've been reluctant up till now to tell others when I am lonely or ask for prayer about it. What if I suddenly have a horde at my doorstep the next day? I'm not looking for people to come out of the woodwork. I don't want or need that. But I do long for someone, or more likely some few, to connect with my soul. Some whose company is fulfilling and deeply satisfying. Sadly, after four marriages, I know that for me this probably isn't to be found in a husband. Though I do, at times, long to hold someone's hand. Put my head on someone's shoulder. Have someone greet me when I arrive home after a long trip—other than Piper, my cat.

I think it is okay to be alone, feel lonely, and experience some loneliness at times. It's part of being human and living life. But we don't have to settle for sad, oppressive loneliness as a permanent condition. I think of Paul writing his letter to the Philippians. Surely, he must have felt loneliness in his cell. Yet he wrote this:

> Rejoice in the Lord always; again I will say, rejoice! Let your gentle spirit be known to all men. The Lord is near. Be anxious for nothing, but in everything by prayer and supplication with thanksgiving let your requests be made known to God. And the peace of God, which surpasses all comprehension, will guard your hearts and your minds in Christ Jesus. (Phil. 4:4–7)

With that passage in mind, I decided I could boldly request of God that He replace my loneliness with what I really longed for: a deeper connection to Him and to others so that I no longer feel lonely. That is the journey I've been on, and it has led me to this book. I'm glad you've joined me on this journey, for I have found it is full of surprises.

One thing I quickly learned is that not all of us mean the same thing when we use certain terms, so for clarity's sake let's agree on a few simple meanings. Naturally, we'll take a closer look at each of these as we move forward, but this will ensure we are on the same page when I use these words.

- *Alone* is neither a negative nor positive word. It simply means physically by oneself. One may or may not *want* to be alone or feel alone, so we always need to look at the context when we use this word.

- *Lonely* and *loneliness* refer to a negative, sad feeling, a longing for companionship, a sense of connection, and a sense of belonging.

- Loneliness can be *circumstantial*, meaning it comes and goes according to the circumstances, or, if left unchecked, can become *chronic*, which means continuing, or occurring again and again, or always present.

- *Solitude*, as I use the word, means a very positive, satisfying choice to be alone. It is restorative and regenerative. We will spend two chapters on this intriguing concept!

- *Isolation*, on the other hand, is used as a negative word to mean keeping apart, separating, withdrawing, and becoming self-focused and self-occupied. It stresses detachment from others and may be voluntary or involuntary.

I have certainly discovered in the writing of this book that I am far from alone in my feeling of loneliness. Whatever type or degree of loneliness you are suffering, you are not alone either.

Maybe you've recently moved into a new area. Your friends and family are no longer just around the corner, available for a shared meal or an enjoyable outing or a quick break at the local coffee shop. You realize that there is no one around who, when they look into your eyes, already knows your story. Everyone is a stranger, and the thought of forging new relationships seems draining and even pointless because there is no one with whom you share a history.

Maybe when you are in a crowd, at the mall or at church or anywhere you are surrounded by people, in spite of all the faces around you, you feel deeply alone. You wear a smile on your face like a mask, but behind that mask is a sad face.

Maybe you've been betrayed or abandoned or divorced. The door has slammed shut on the relationship that you once trusted would last a lifetime, and you are left alone. You are alone.

Maybe you are struggling in your marriage. You close the bedroom door, and you are alone in the room. You can't get away from the loneliness that fills your house and your heart.

Maybe you are in a new job and feel that no one has your back. You aren't sure who you can trust, and it's hard imagining breaking through the polite niceties to real connections.

Maybe, no matter what your circumstances, you feel invisible. "Not to be seen is to feel cursed. . . . Many experience this sense of invisibility," writes Trevor Hudson.[2] There is no lonelier feeling. There are countless life scenarios that can leave someone feeling lonely, and so there are many people just like you and me. Take Cindy, for example.

Cindy took a deep breath to try to calm her emotions before climbing out of her car with the baby shower gift and walking up the sidewalk to Terri's front door. Another baby shower. *How many showers have I been to in the six years I've been trying to have a baby of my own?* she thought. *Too many!* She wasn't proud of her foul mood and had to remind herself that she was here not out of obligation but out of genuine friendship with Terri. Still, this was her first shower since her miscarriage six months ago, and though she'd felt she could handle coming, now she wasn't so sure.

As the door opened, Cindy pasted on her best effort of a genuine smile and stepped into a living room filled with women talking and laughing. She made her way through the room, giving a few hugs to friends and warm hellos to strangers all while trying to scope out a seat on the edges so she wouldn't have to engage in much small talk. Just as she set her gift with the others, she spotted a folding chair squeezed into a back corner behind the couch. Perfect. Now to make her way through the mingling crowd, past the table displaying the sheet cake decorated in pink and blue roses and the pretty stack of party favors wrapped in yellow netting with pink and blue ribbons. An unwelcome question pushed itself to the front of her thinking: *Pink or blue? Was the baby I lost a girl or a boy? I don't even know that much.* She swallowed hard, trying to push the thought from her mind, and finally took her seat.

Though surrounded by women, Cindy felt painfully lonely. In truth, given the statistics of miscarriages, she probably had that in common with at least several other women in the room, but no one shares those stories at a shower. The talk buzzing around her was of birth stories and potty training and feeding routines and milestones like first steps and first words. Stories Cindy knew she might never have of her own. As the party wore on and adorable baby gifts were passed around the circle of guests, Cindy played her part in the oohing and aahing while her loneliness deepened.

Cindy spotted a clock on the wall. She tried not to be obvious as she checked the time over and over again. *How long*, she wondered, *until the gifts have all been opened and the cake served? Then I can get out of here!*

Though I've never shared Cindy's circumstances, I can relate to her so easily. I know what it is like to be surrounded by people yet feel desperately lonely. To feel alone in my suffering when those around me seem to have so much to celebrate. I found an Elisabeth Elliot quote that captures this experience perfectly. You may resonate with it as well.

Elisabeth Elliot was a renowned author, speaker, and missionary I have greatly admired. As a Christian woman she was certainly more than qualified to write about loneliness. In 1956 her first husband, Jim Elliot, was killed while attempting to make missionary contact with the Auca Indians of Ecuador. She later spent two years as a missionary to the very tribe that killed her husband, and she also spent many years as a single missionary in South America. She was widowed again in 1973 after spending only four years as the wife of Dr. Addison Leitch. She wrote, "In the wilderness of loneliness we are terribly vulnerable. We want OUT."[3]

Yes. Exactly! OUT. Those of us who know the pain and longing of loneliness don't want a to-do list or a pep talk or a chart of ten things to do to make new friends, and we certainly don't want to be told to just enjoy our solitude. We want out of the ache we feel, and we want out *now*.

Encounter in the Wilderness

There is a woman whose story is told in the book of Genesis who also wanted out—desperately. Her name is Hagar. I love her story because of what we discover about loneliness and God as He intervenes in her life.

Hagar had been purchased as a slave from Egypt, which at the time was a very cultured society that worshiped many gods. She had probably been ripped from her family against her will, taken from all she knew and loved. A very well-to-do nomadic family took her as a servant for the lady of the home, Sarai. She and her husband, Abram (Abram and Sarai are later renamed by God as Abraham and Sarah), had also come from a pagan culture—the Canaanites. God had previously called Abram to leave his homeland and follow Him, promising him that not only would He make a great nation out of Abram but that his descendants would outnumber the stars.

As the property of Abram and Sarai, Hagar had nothing in her life that was her own. She had no choice but to obey and serve her masters. In many ways, Hagar was all alone as this large family group traveled to an unknown, distant country. Oh, she was surrounded by other servants, but ultimately she was alone—without family or friends or culture familiar to her. No one was there to care for her, comfort her, or dry her tears. She may have been frightened or confused, with no idea what her future held—or even if she had a future.

Abram was a man of considerable means, rich in livestock, silver, and gold, so at least Hagar would have been living comfortably amid this nomadic lifestyle. Along the way, the company and possessions grew, and as Sarai's maidservant, it's likely Hagar saw her responsibilities grow as well. But a comfortable lifestyle and many people do not negate loneliness of the heart.

It was no secret that the couple believed their God's promises of a child and the eventual nation to come through him. And yet, month after month, year after year, the longed-for, promised child never became a reality. As the years passed and the couple approached one hundred years old, the more unlikely this possibility became. I wonder what the rest of the company thought about all this hope. Did they believe in Abram's God? (There is no evidence Hagar believed.) Did they snicker at this crazy idea? After all, this couple was far too old to have children. Sarai certainly began to question this word from God.

Eventually Sarai grew tired of waiting for God to fulfill His promise and began to think of a way she could help God out. She took matters into her own hands and ordered Hagar to go into Abram's tent to conceive a baby in her place. To our thinking, this seems weird and perverted. But in that day and age this was accepted as a way to have children to carry on the family line.

How did Hagar feel about this? Scripture doesn't tell us. Perhaps she wanted to help her mistress achieve the goal of having Abram's child to carry on the family heritage. Perhaps she considered it a privilege to serve her mistress in such a way and, if successful, knew this would most likely elevate her status as well. Or perhaps she resented being placed in this role.

Indeed she did get pregnant. Then things began to change. Big time! Hagar, once she had conceived, now despised Sarai. So what did Sarai do? She blamed Abram, who in frustration threw up his hands and said, "Behold, your maid is in your power; do to her what is good in your sight" (Gen. 16:6).

Sarai took out all her disappointment, anger, and hurt on Hagar. After all, Hagar was just a servant. She had no one to protect her. Did she feel betrayed by Sarai and Abram? She had only done what her mistress had commanded, and now she was being attacked. Who would defend her? She had no one. Other servants she had befriended over the years in Abram's caravan would probably not stand up for her, as they wouldn't want to jeopardize their own position. And at this point they probably didn't even want to be seen with her for fear of reprisals from Sarai, who must have been a formidable woman.

Hagar was all alone. The only thing she could think to do was run away. Get out—away from Sarai. She was so desperate that she fled into the wilderness alone. The wilderness is barren. Unfriendly. Dangerous. All sorts of creepy crawlies and strange noises at night. No comforts of home. No protection. No one to talk to—not even another servant. She was alone. Very alone.

Or so it seemed.

In truth, God was watching. We are told that, "the angel of the LORD found her by a spring of water in the wilderness" (v. 7). What happened next was crucial.

In verse 8, the angel asked her, "Hagar, Sarai's maid, where have you come from and where are you going?"

This angel knew her by name! Can you imagine her shock? And the questions he asked weren't because he needed the information. He knew the answers. He wanted her to acknowledge the truth.

Hagar was honest.

She said, "I am fleeing from the presence of my mistress Sarai." Then the angel of the LORD said to her, "Return to your mistress, and submit yourself to her authority." Moreover, the angel of the LORD said to her, "I will greatly multiply your descendants so that they will be too many to count." (vv. 8–10)

Not only did God see her in her desperation and loneliness, and not only did He call her by name, but He gave her a marvelous promise of more descendants than could be counted. And then He topped it all off with the incredible news that she was pregnant with a son.

That would be fantastic news for a woman like Hagar. She wouldn't be alone! And now she knew God saw her and her suffering.

Hagar's response really speaks to me in my own loneliness. She gave God a name. "Then she called the name of the LORD who spoke to her, 'You are a God who sees'" (v. 13). In Hebrew, that name is *El Roi.*

And He is the God who sees us too! When we are lonely and have reached the end of our resources, it is comforting to know God *sees* us. We are not forgotten. He is paying attention. He not only sees us but knows us, and He cares when we feel lost in the harsh wilderness of our loneliness.

Our Rescue Is on the Way

Hagar discovered something else about the God of Abraham that day—something that is true for you and me as well. Not only did He see her and know her and care about her but *He had a plan for her.* A plan that far exceeded anything she could have ever hoped for as a slave. In Hagar's unique situation, not only would she have a son but she would have innumerable descendants. His plan for you and me will be unique to our lives as well, but rest assured, God does have a plan for you.

As God's Word says, "'For I know the plans I have for you,' declares the LORD, 'plans to prosper you and not to harm you, plans to give you hope and a future'" (Jer. 29:11 NIV). For Hagar's plan to unfold, however, she had to follow God's instruction, and what He asked of her was not easy. She was told to return to Sarai and submit to her authority. Ouch. Hagar's struggles weren't over. She had more ahead of her. But the difference now was that rather than lose herself in the emptiness of the wilderness, she could *invest* herself in following God's direction, knowing He had a plan for her. This gave her hope. This gave her a reason to endure.

And that is why I am sharing Hagar's story near the beginning of this book. I want to encourage you, in the midst of your loneliness, to endure in the certain hope that God has a plan for you that is now unfolding. You may not yet know where that plan will lead, but knowing He *sees* you, *knows* you, and *has a plan* for you is great solid ground for the beginning of your journey to having God transform your loneliness. So, too, is the understanding that God loves you so much that He *intervenes* in your life to call you to follow Him.

As you think through what that means in light of how lonely you are, also think about how you would answer the two questions the angel posed to Hagar.

Where have you come from?

Where are you going?

I hope you know you have come from the loving hand of the Creator God, who formed you in your mother's womb. I hope you are headed to an eternity with Jesus in heaven with God the Father. If you believe in Jesus as your Lord and Savior, that is the big picture of your story! Everything else that is part of your story falls between those two immovable points.

If we look back at Cindy's story, we see she was coming from a painful miscarriage. Where was she headed? That looked uncertain. All she seemed to know in that moment was that she felt lost and wanted out of the loneliness of that baby shower. But what if she knew God's unique future for her? Though it would be years yet before He revealed it to her, God was going to have Cindy adopt an at-risk eight-year-old boy who desperately needed a loving Christian mother. And one day, through a series of unexpected surprises, she would become a mother of six and grandmother of ten! God was also going to use her to counsel many women through the painful journeys of infertility, miscarriage, and adoption. God had a truly beautiful plan in store for her. It was a plan that would eventually lead her to being more deeply connected with God and with others than ever before. And *that* was going to truly relieve and satisfy her loneliness.

How do we move from feeling lost in our loneliness to being where we long to be—more deeply connected to God and to others? We learn to watch for God to show up and *intervene* in our lives when we are lost in our loneliness!

Lost and Found

I can still vividly recall a time when I was lost—physically lost—though it happened decades ago. I was driving from my home in Philadelphia to Washington, DC, to babysit my nephew at a hotel while his parents went to an event at the White House. I knew where I needed to be (this was way before GPS). But as anyone who has ever driven in DC will attest, it is more than difficult to navigate.

On my first try I came pretty close to my destination—the hotel. In fact, I could see it not far away. I thought I could circle the block and reach it. Not in DC! You think you are going around the block, but then you hit a roundabout and the street you were on is no longer the same street. And when you try to get back to it, you hit a one-way street that angles diagonally away from the street you were on. The harder I tried to get back on track, the farther away I moved from my destination. I did this for at least two hours! (Thank goodness I'd allowed extra time.) It was getting dark. I was circling ever wider and getting nowhere fast, and I found myself in a bad part of town. I was becoming anxious and more than a little frustrated.

Finally, I saw a policeman and stopped to ask him how to get to where I needed to be. He patiently explained to me how to navigate DC, and I arrived just in time to see my sister and brother-in-law head to the White House. (By the way, I've since been told DC was mapped out by L'Enfant, who designed it so that cannon balls could not be shot down the streets in a straight line. Maybe so, but he did modern drivers no favors!)

Being lost is frightening.

Jesus told a parable about a lost sheep. Apparently, he had wandered off, as sheep are wont to do. If the sheep had been in a wide, green pasture, it would not have been so bad. But the land Jesus was talking about was rough. Pasture was scarce. Often a bit of pasture was bordered by a ravine. It was dangerous territory. The shepherd had to be vigilant and keep watch night and day, for he was personally responsible for his sheep. He was there to lead his sheep—they are followers. He was there to protect his sheep—they are helpless.

He was there to defend his sheep—they are defenseless. They have no claws or teeth. They have no speed.

This sheep kept munching along, following his mouth, unconcerned about where he was going. When he finally looked up, he was alone—all alone. Where was the flock? He didn't know. Where was the shepherd? He couldn't see anything familiar. He was frightened. He didn't know what to do.

Without food and water and protection the sheep was in peril. Was he bleating? Perhaps it was his bleating that alerted his shepherd. Had he fallen and injured himself? Were coyotes circling him, ready to pounce? Was the sheep exhausted in his efforts or too dumb to notice where he was?

But then, as he raised his eyes to the horizon, he saw a familiar figure bounding toward him—his shepherd!

Without hesitation, the shepherd had left the ninety-nine to search out the one sheep that was lost and in need. It was dangerous for the shepherd too. But he didn't care about the cost to himself. He went after the missing sheep.

When the shepherd reached the sheep, he didn't scold or berate him. Instead he lifted him upon his shoulders and carried the no-longer-lost sheep home with him. He was safe and secure.

Just as I was glad to reach the hotel that night and glad to be surrounded by family, a warm meal, and security, I imagine the sheep felt the same on his shepherd's shoulders. And once safely back, the shepherd rejoiced to have the lost one back in the fold.

Being lost is frightening. Being lost and alone is very frightening. But we have a shepherd who comes to rescue us. Though we may feel alone and lost in the wilderness, our rescuer is already on the way.

Be assured that you are in relationship with the One who created you and knows you best and loves you most. He sees you. He knows you. He has a plan for you. And He intervenes in your life—in fact, He is already on the way.

Hold tight and keep your eyes open for His coming!

Wait for the LORD;
Be strong and let your heart take courage;
Yes, wait for the LORD.

Psalm 27:14

The Best of Company

God comes looking for us. God continues to pursue our
companionship.

Trevor Hudson[1]

Over the past several years, multiple research studies and
hundreds—if not thousands—of articles have focused on
the topic of loneliness. The common thread always points
to a lack of connectedness, of community, of belonging.
While some disagreement among experts exists regarding
whether or not loneliness is a "growing" problem or not, or
even an "epidemic" or not, no one seems to disagree that
a large percentage of people in the world today are lonely.
And not just a little lonely! *Very* lonely.

In preparation for this book, I dove into the research for
myself to see what I could discover about the prevalence of
loneliness, its causes and cures, the toll it takes, and even the
possible benefits it may bring. I also collected meaningful
quotes from various experts because I love the power of a

wise quote to challenge our thinking and lift our perspectives from our own limited viewpoints to see the larger picture. I confess, at first the more research I did on loneliness, the more discouraged I became. (You'll discover why in chapter 5.) In the face of such staggering statistics and dismal reports, I had to wonder, How hopeless is the condition of loneliness? Is it simply part of the human condition that we need to resign ourselves to? Should we just accept it, buck up, grit our teeth, and bear it?

And then I came across a quote from an expert that put it all in perspective. The quote was part of an extensive document that gave a complete history of loneliness, from its beginnings long ago to its future. Here is the quote:

> It is not good for the man to be alone.

You may recognize it. The expert is God. The document is the Bible. This quote is Genesis 2:18, to be exact. And its message is clear. Being alone is *not* a good thing. (No wonder we hate the feeling so much!) Therefore, it is a condition that needs to be remedied. And to understand its remedy, we need to understand its origin. In fact, we need to understand *our* origin.

God Enjoys Living in Community

Have you ever puzzled over this verse? "Let Us make man in Our image, according to Our likeness" (Gen. 1:26). Why is God speaking of Himself in the plural? Because God Himself lives in community. He is the Trinity—Father, Son, and Holy Spirit. Jesus was one with God and the Holy Spirit when He

44

laid the foundations of the earth, measuring it out. He was even there before all of that. Creation was actually a Father and Son project. Speaking of Jesus, Colossians 1:15–19 says,

> He is the image of the invisible God, the firstborn of all creation. For by Him all things were created, both in the heavens and on earth, visible and invisible, whether thrones or dominions or rulers or authorities—all things have been created through Him and for Him. He is before all things, and in Him all things hold together. . . . For it was the Father's good pleasure for all the fullness to dwell in Him.

The Father and Son enjoy one another. I can only imagine how God's creative juices flowed as they came up with the aardvark or platypus. They must have had a sense of humor! And how they came up with the design for each snowflake. Intricate. Unique. Delicate. Fragile. The triune God is the Master Artist from whom all true artists draw their inspiration. God and Jesus delighted in one another. Constantly in each other's company. Creating. Planning. Enjoying.

And yet as He looked around at all He created, it wasn't complete. He wanted someone to walk in the garden with Him. Someone to cooperate with Him in tending the garden and the animals. Someone to worship Him.

So when God, who has always lived in community, created us in His image, He designed us, like Him, to live in community as well. We were built for community. It's in our DNA. God did not create us to be alone. We are made for relationship. That is why loneliness can be so painful. I once heard Bishop James C. Hash Sr. of St. Peter's Church and World Outreach Center say, "The truth is, while God designed us for a fulfilling relationship with Him, He also said it isn't good for us to be alone. In fact, He says it in the second chapter of Genesis. Adam had God to commune with, and he had plenty of animals. Yet neither God nor animals filled quite the same role as another person could, so God created Eve to be his helpmate, friend and more."

Did Adam even realize he was alone before God called it to his attention? I wonder. "He was enjoying his fellowship with God. But God saw that Adam needed a friend, helper and companion."[2] A companion more like Adam—Eve! They enjoyed fellowship with God together—the three of them.

Sadly, Adam and Eve broke that perfect fellowship with God by disobeying Him in eating the forbidden fruit. The next thing we know is that God came to visit them in the garden. I love that God came seeking out their companionship! But rather than joyfully running toward their Creator, they hid from Him because they were ashamed. And so began the separation of humankind from our Creator.

But He did not leave it at that. God knew how He had created us, and that friendship with God is essential to our souls. Separation of humanity from Him was so intolerable to God that He chose to restore the relationship through sending His Son to earth to reconcile us to Him. But the cost—to God—was great. First, the Trinity would have to endure Jesus's departure from heaven. They had always been together in the heavenly realm. One can only imagine the loneliness God felt as Jesus went to earth to be born as a baby. Have you ever packed your firstborn off to summer camp, college, or boot camp? That might give you a hint. God was putting His heart "out there" for sinners. He knew that earth wasn't a safe place. He sent Jesus because He loved us and wanted to redeem us for Himself. This was His plan all along, but it cost Him the constant companionship of His beloved only Son. Like the song "What a Beautiful Name It Is" says, He "didn't want heaven without us." So God endured the loneliness of Jesus's absence from heaven. I don't know if that is theologically correct, but think about it. They had always been connected, an integral part of each other. And now . . .

But that separation wasn't the only cost. It was merely the beginning. God watched from heaven as His adored Son was brutalized by those who didn't know or want to know that God's kingdom was different from how they'd envisioned it. There must have been a hush over heaven. All the busyness came to a halt. Did the angels fold their wings and silence their choruses? I imagine it must have been quiet. Deadly quiet. The Father's heart was being torn asunder. Did a tear roll down His face? As the nails went through Jesus's hands and feet, surely God felt the pain. His head crowned in glory must have felt the thorns thrust onto the head of His Son. God felt it all because they are one.

Jesus, the darling of heaven, was not by His side. He was suffering, alone, on the cross. Yes, He knew what was coming. He knew resurrection was just a few days away. Yet His heart broke. He endured that loneliness for us.

When we love, we open ourselves up for hurt. God did. He loved us and we rejected Him. We wanted our own way. We spurned His message. His love. His presence. We killed His exact representation to us. And the Father, knowing all of that would take place, sent His Son to us anyway. Why? Because He loved us and wanted to restore the fellowship— the community, the connection—between us and God.

Jesus Endures Ultimate Loneliness

If that is what the Father felt, what about the Son? Jesus, too, endured the separation of Himself from the godhead to be sent to earth and live among men. What was it like to go from the glory of heaven to the rough hay of a smelly manger? What was it like to relinquish His heavenly body for the tiny body of a helpless, dependent infant? We cannot fathom it.

I find it fascinating, however, to witness the decisions Jesus made to model for us how vitally important connection, community, and belonging truly are, for in His earthly ministry we see Him not going it alone (surely He could have!) but choosing to build relationships—close and meaningful relationships—to accomplish His work on earth. Just as He and His Father had chosen to work together on creation, so Jesus chose to work together with His chosen followers in His earthly ministry. We know He chose the twelve disciples. Yet He also chose among those twelve to have an especially close bond with Peter, James, and John. And among those three He chose John as His closest friend. Beyond the twelve, we see in Luke 10:1 that Jesus chose seventy-two "and sent them in pairs ahead of Him to every city and place where He Himself was going to come." Clearly as the Son of God He *could* have worked alone, but He didn't *choose* to work alone. He chose to work in community.

We'll explore more about Jesus's relationships in coming chapters. For now, let's focus on the day Jesus paid the penalty for our sins: the day of the crucifixion. For once Jesus was betrayed and arrested in the Garden of Gethsemane and His disciples fled, Jesus was totally *alone*. How lonely must He have been when arrested by rough soldiers with swords and clubs and led away to the high priest, all the chief priests, the elders, and the scribes? How deep was His loneliness as He endured so many people falsely accusing Him? What was it like to stand alone in the face of a crowd condemning Him as deserving of death, spitting on Him, blindfolding Him, beating Him with their fists, and daring Him to prophesy?

But that was only the beginning, wasn't it? Next He was bound and handed over to Pilate to endure questioning—all alone. Alone He endured the crowd chanting angrily, "Crucify Him! Crucify Him!" Then He was mercilessly flogged. Then mocked and abused by the Roman soldiers before being taken away, carrying His cross on His back, to be crucified. Finally He was thrown down upon that cross naked, His arms stretched wide and His loving hands held open while nails were driven through His wrists and then His feet. Humiliated. Alone.

Yes, Jesus willingly endured agonizing pain and loneliness, until finally, "about the ninth hour Jesus cried out with a loud voice, saying . . . 'My God, My God, why have You forsaken Me?'" (Matt. 27:46). The moment had come. It was a moment unlike any other He had experienced in all eternity. Utter loneliness. As the sin of the world bore down on His broken body, Jesus endured the ultimate loneliness: separation from God.

My heart would break for the horror of it, except for an important Scripture that puts it all into perspective. Jesus's perspective.

Let us run with endurance the race that is set before us, fixing our eyes on Jesus, the author and perfecter of faith, who for the joy set before Him endured the cross, despising the shame, and has sat down at the right hand of the throne of God. (Heb. 12:1–2)

Did you catch that? The motivation that pushed Jesus to endure such torture? *The joy set before Him.*

What was that joy?

It all goes back to the Garden of Eden. To that painful separation, that breaking of perfect fellowship between God and man. The separation that so grieved God, that so violated the way God had designed us to live in fellowship with Him. God had set this entire plan in motion and Jesus had willingly stepped up to pay the price . . . to do what? "He has now reconciled you in His fleshly body through death, in order to present you before Him holy and blameless and beyond reproach" (Col. 1:22).

The joy set before Jesus Christ was to present us holy and blameless to His Father so that we might once again be in fellowship with God the Father, God the Son, and God the Holy Spirit. A grand reunion! The ultimate end of all loneliness.

Your Personal Invitation

Before turning even one more page of this book, I want you to ask yourself some questions: Will you be at that grand reunion? You can know for sure. Will Jesus one day present you to God as pure and blameless and beyond reproach? You make that choice this side of heaven. Do you know Jesus Christ as your Lord and personal Savior? If you have any doubt at all—even the tiniest of doubts—I invite you to turn to appendix A at the back of this book. For loneliness on this earth is one thing. It's a big thing and we are going to spend the rest of this book exploring what to do about it. But earthly loneliness is *temporary*. The most important step you can take right now is to ensure you will not suffer *eternal* loneliness. Friendship with God is essential to your eternal soul.

You Are in Good Company

As I hope you now see, if you know the pain of loneliness—and want out of it—you are in some very good company. In fact, the very best of company. God knows what it is like to be separated from the fellowship of the people He created. He wanted out of that eternal separation so badly He was willing to endure separation from His own Son so our fellowship could be restored. Jesus knows loneliness too. He's felt it at its very worst. Yet He was willing to endure it to save us from eternal separation from God.

The Bible is filled with stories of others who have endured loneliness as well—and from what I can see, they all wanted out of it. They didn't want to be lonely. Consider Hagar, Jonah, Moses, Noah, Daniel, Job, Zacchaeus, Peter, Paul, and Silas. I had never before done a study of loneliness in the Bible, and I came away from it surprised and challenged. I believe those of us who know the pain of loneliness will see the stories of these flesh-and-blood people and our own loneliness experiences in an entirely new light.

Of course we don't have to only dip into the distant past to find ourselves in the good company of lonely people. Lori, Kathy, Alison, Brittany, Elle, Liz, Meg, Kori, Lynn, and others each willingly allowed me to share their stories of loneliness. I believe you'll find value in each of their experiences.

And of course, I explore my own lonely experiences as well and share my discovery that time and spiritual growth since those events have dramatically altered my understanding of what I'd experienced. I hope the same will be true for you.

Finally, I'm looking forward to revealing to you the comments, experiences, perceptions, and realities of a huge host—thousands upon many thousands—of people from around the world who participated in loneliness research studies in just the past few years. I have no doubt that if you have ever suffered loneliness, you will find yourself in at least a few and perhaps many of the responses given. What a unique glimpse into the world God sees, knows, and loves. I pray that as you peer into the hidden places of so many hearts you will be moved, as I have been, with insight, compassion, a sense of belonging to the larger family of God, and who knows what else? Perhaps even a fresh mission and newfound purpose. I know I will never look at a crowd large or small—be it at church, at the grocery store, at a stadium, or in line at the post office—the same way again.

Equipped with an Eternal Perspective

You and I, like all of humanity, were designed for community in the image of God. In this lonely world, however, that community is fractured. From the time that first sweet relationship between God and man was broken, God set in place His eternal plan—and you and I are going to need to keep that eternal perspective as we move through the next chapters in this book and the coming chapters of our lives.

We began this chapter in Genesis. How perfect, then, to end it in Revelation:

Behold, the tabernacle of God is among men, and He will dwell among them, and they shall be His people, and God Himself will be among them, and He will wipe away every tear from their eyes; and there will no longer be any death; there will no longer be any mourning, or crying, or pain; the first things have passed away. (21:3–4)

Let's also hold fast to the fact that God is not only involved in what happens in our eternal future. God is deeply involved in our present reality! The very next verse says it all. Notice that it is in the present tense, rather than the future tense, and I pray for it to be the opening verse to your next experience with this book.

And He who sits on the throne said, "Behold, I am making all things new."

Revelation 21:5

4

The Well-Kept Secret

To combat loneliness, we must first learn how to identify it and
to have the courage to see that experience as a warning sign.

Brené Brown[1]

I came across some good news about loneliness recently. Some
truly excellent news!

It was the title of the article that caught my eye: "In the
Midst of the Pandemic, Loneliness Has Leveled Out." At
first, I thought it was one of those sly, misleading titles
designed just to pull you in with a hopeful promise before
delivering more bad news. (I don't like being a skeptic, but
after a year of reading about and researching loneliness
I've grown accustomed to bad news on the subject.) But
sure enough, the title was true. By late summer of 2020,
after many months of loneliness caused by the COVID-19
pandemic lockdowns, several studies revealed that loneliness worldwide was leveling off.

"Before the coronavirus pandemic, there was a loneliness
epidemic," wrote Kasley Killam, in *Scientific American*.

By some estimates, two thirds of Americans often or always felt lonely in 2019. So when quarantines and shelter-in-place orders began, I was one of many social scientists who raised concerns that loneliness might worsen in the months to come. Would prolonged isolation trigger a "social recession," as former US surgeon general Vivek H. Murthy and physician Alice T. Chen put it?[2]

A number of studies, including one in the United States, one in the United Kingdom, and one in Germany, all had similar results indicating that during the worldwide lockdowns sudden isolation had triggered a spike in loneliness, but people quickly adapted and found ways to maintain social connection despite the circumstances. For many, it seems, their appreciation of it was heightened. Many people prioritized such connection. There was a surge in volunteerism. People used technology to maintain personal relationships. Killam concluded the article with these hopeful words:

> We all feel powerless when it comes to the coronavirus, but we still have some control over our social lives and our social health. We can call our loved ones, participate in quarantine pods, reach out to isolated neighbors and organize virtual gatherings. Now is the time to strengthen bonds within families, neighborhoods and communities of all kinds—because by doing so, we will not only endure; we might emerge better off.[3]

It wasn't happening on its own, of course, like some virus running its course. No, it was happening because people started practicing some of what this book proposes.

I've been seeing this borne out in my neighborhood as neighbors have gathered each Saturday at 10:00 out on the community lawn, reaching out to each other. They socially distance in their lawn chairs and visit. And that brings me to this chapter. I want to give you an opportunity through these pages to "visit" with other lonely people around the world who have taken part in a wide variety of loneliness research. But first, here's some more news.

In May 2019, *Forbes* magazine reported that,

> alarming statistics about loneliness [are] now accompanied by equally alarming warnings that loneliness is stunting our lives and outright killing us. . . . A recent Cigna survey revealed that nearly half of Americans always or sometimes feel alone (46%) or left out (47%).[4]

Nearly *half*? That's a shockingly high percentage! And such figures have frequently been in the press in the couple of years leading up to this book.

The Cigna survey also shows that more than half of respondents—54 percent—said they sometimes or always felt like no one knows them well, and 56 percent reported they sometimes or always felt like the people around them "are not necessarily with them." Two in five felt like "they lack companionship," their "relationships aren't meaningful," and they "are isolated from others."[5]

What is this Cigna survey? Well, the health insurer Cigna surveyed twenty thousand adults across the United States using a highly respected tool for measuring loneliness: the UCLA Loneliness Scale. Would you like to see the twenty questions on the survey? Better yet, would you like to see where you fit on this scale?

I invite you to use the same tool. You will find it in appendix B. All you need is a pencil or a pen. This chapter will mean more to you if you pause your reading to take the survey now.

Scores on this loneliness scale can range from 20 to 80. A score of 43 and above was interpreted as "lonely" in the Cigna survey, and higher scores indicated an even greater level of loneliness and social isolation. The survey found that the average loneliness score in America is 44. That means most Americans are considered lonely! And as we'll explore shortly, loneliness is certainly not a distinctly American issue.

I would like to give you enough information to recognize the key loneliness issues that trouble people and to allow you to explore those same issues for yourself. Then, as we continue through the book, you'll better recognize the value and usefulness of the principles we'll be exploring.

So, looking back over the data in the few preceding paragraphs, let's make some personal observations.

Do you always or often feel lonely? Nearly half of Americans feel that way.

Do you lack companionship? Do you feel that your relationships aren't meaningful? Do you feel left out or isolated? If you are in a group of five people—let's say at your local restaurant—it's likely two in that group would say yes to all three questions.

Do you always or sometimes feel that no one knows you well? Well, guess what? More than half of Americans feel that way too.

Do you have meaningful in-person social interactions on a daily basis, such as having an extended conversation with a friend or spending time with family members? According to the Cigna study, only around half of Americans say they do.

Are you getting the picture? Loneliness is the well-kept secret of so many people you know. You'd never be able to tell just by looking around, but you are literally surrounded by people who are struggling just as you are.

Who's in This with You?

Let's start by identifying which generation you fall into.

- Greatest Generation: born prior to 1944
- Baby Boomers: born 1944–1964
- Gen X: born 1965–1979
- Millennials: born 1980–1994
- Gen Z: born 1995–2015

Research seems to indicate that issues with loneliness are most pronounced among Gen Z, then Millennials, then older Baby Boomers. Gen X and younger Baby Boomers tag along as less lonely. Though which generation is the loneliest seems to fluctuate by survey, my reading indicated that most concluded Gen Z was the loneliest generation of all.[6]

Consider this:

> The effects of social disconnection (neglect, strain, isolation) or connection (supportive, stable family environment) that occurred earlier in life will become more apparent later in life. Further, there are a number of important life transitions among older adults that may result in disruptions or decreases in social connection (e.g., retirement, widowhood, children leaving home, age-related health problems).[7]

Greatest Generation (born prior to 1944)

- Those born prior to 1944 ranked as the least lonely, with a score of 38.6.[8] However, adults over age seventy-five were more susceptible to becoming lonely due to life factors such as declining health or the loss of a spouse or significant other. Social isolation among the elderly remains a huge problem that will only grow worse as Baby Boomers age.[9]

Baby Boomers (born 1944–1964)

- The total number of older adults who are lonely may increase once Baby Boomers reach their late seventies and eighties.[10]
- When asked, "How often do you feel lonely?" statistics report that Baby Boomers say "always" or "often" 15 percent of the time.[11]

Gen X (born 1965–1979)

- Gen X had a loneliness score of 45.1.
- When asked, "How often do you feel lonely?" statistics report that Gen X says "always" or "often" 20 percent of the time.[12]

Millennials (born 1980–1994)

- Millennials, with a loneliness score of 45.3, were close behind Gen X.
- Here's a sad number: more than one in five Millennials (22 percent) in a recent YouGov poll said they had "zero friends," 27 percent said they had "no

close friends," and 30 percent said they had "no best friends."[13]

- When asked, "How often do you feel lonely?" statistics report that Millennials say "always" or "often" 30 percent of the time.[14]

Gen Z (born 1995–2015)

- Gen Z was the loneliest generation, with a loneliness score of 48.3.
- Citing the Cigna study, *Psychology Today* reported that Gen Z was found to be the loneliest generation of all. We might be tempted to blame this on that generation's use of social media, but according to that report, not so: "social media use alone is not a predictor of loneliness."[15] My twenty-three-year-old grandson may see it differently. He texted me,

> Our generation is super lonely. We're so connected, but a lot of people can't connect outside of online. Johann Hari, author of *Lost Connections*, says that more than half of Americans don't have an emergency contact to reach in a time of need. It's strange: we have a lot of interactions but not many meaningful interactions.

- He went on to text, "It's scary, but it'll get better once people learn to live happily and healthily with technology. I hope." He bears out the statistics that younger people report a lack of companionship.
- This was an eye-opening quote for me to read and shows a real shift in our culture from previous generations:

Adolescence is no longer characterized by a growing desire for independence. According to Jean Twenge, the number of teenagers who get together with their friends nearly every day has dropped 40 percent since 2000. One teenager described this phenomenon simply: "I think we like our phones more than we like actual people." Not only does this make for more lonely teenagers, it also hinders their social, emotional, and psychological development. A lack of interaction now will make it significantly harder for these young people to begin new relationships, interview for jobs, navigate courtship, and build healthy families in their adult life.[16]

Before we move on, here's a sobering thought for all of us, no matter which generation we fall into: among the elderly, social isolation causes a huge loneliness problem. That gives us all fair warning that we'd better build solutions into our lives now so we can cope with challenges as we age. What will happen, for instance, to Gen Z and Millennials, who are already reporting such high levels of loneliness, as they reach old age?

What Are the Symptoms?

I had some questions of my own about loneliness, and I wanted to survey some people who had lots of experience with it. I am so grateful to a group of military spouses who kindly responded to my questions. You will find wisdom from them scattered throughout this book.

One of the first things I asked them was, "Describe how you feel when you are lonely." See if you recognize yourself in any of these answers.

- "Loneliness feels like hopelessness. This feeling persists most heavily when circumstances are trying."
- "It feels like the world is falling apart and no one cares."
- "I feel like there is an important element missing in my life."
- "Isolated, unknown, unneeded, frustrated, discouraged."
- "Sad, jealous of others near family and childhood friends."
- "Hurting. Alone. Bored. Depressed."
- "I feel down and sometimes wonder if it is something about me that keeps me from connecting with others."
- "I feel like an outsider. Not quite in the loop."
- "Loneliness is paralyzing and blinding. You try to fill it with other things—but nothing replaces community."
- "Heavy, sloth-like, and tired."
- "Sad, pessimistic for the future, unworthy."
- "Empty, like I could cry at any moment."
- "Unseen."

Where Are You From?

Is the loneliness problem primarily in America? All the respondents to the Cigna study were Americans. What about those in other nations? As I've mentioned, the plague of loneliness is spread far wider than US borders. Author Dennis Prager writes,

As social commentator Kay Hymowitz wrote in *City Journal* in 2019 . . . Germans are lonely, the bon vivant French are lonely, and even the Scandinavians—the happiest people in the world, according to the UN's World Happiness Report—are lonely, too . . . consider Japan, a country now in the throes of an epidemic of *kodokushi*, roughly translated as "lonely deaths." Local Japanese papers regularly publish stories about kinless elderly whose deaths go unnoticed until the telltale smell of maggot-eaten flesh alerts neighbors.[17]

In October 2018 the BBC released a nationwide survey reporting that 30 percent of Britons responded that they were often or very often lonely.[18] The British prime minister, Theresa May, clearly took the massive problem of loneliness quite seriously. She appointed a Minister of Loneliness to take point on addressing this critical issue. I also found that "in Canada, the share of solo households is now 28%. Across the European Union, it's 34%."[19] And I was shocked to read, "In Japan, there are more than half a million people under 40 who haven't left their house or interacted with anyone for at least six months."[20] What? How can that be? I cannot fathom so many desperately lonely people in one nation!

Why Are You Lonely?

"What is driving us to self-destruction?" asked author and researcher Francie Hart Broghammer. "There are many factors, all with one unifying theme: We are no longer living in community with one another and, consequently, we are lonely."[21]

Over the year I worked on this book, people often asked me what topic I was writing on. When I answered that the book was on loneliness, I would frequently get this question: "Why do you think it is that loneliness has become such a major problem in today's world?" I enjoyed making the most of the opportunity to do some informal research of my own by asking the same question back to them: "Why do *you* believe that loneliness is running rampant?" This often led people to open up to me about the loneliness they felt and the reasons they thought they might feel that way.

I don't for a moment want to give the impression that I hold the answer to this complex question of why loneliness is so widespread today. As I've seen just from my own reading, there are a host of qualified experts around the world delving into research trying to discover just that. My own inclination is to better understand the spiritual reasons for loneliness, which I traced in chapter 3 by going back to Genesis and focusing on the fall.

But there are also cultural and societal reasons at work in today's world that might explain why loneliness seems to be rising to what many experts consider to be epidemic levels. I'd like to focus on just four big reasons:

1. Geographic mobility
2. Technology
3. Decrease in common cultural connections
   a. There is a change in family makeup.
   b. The size, makeup, and availability of community organizations have dramatically shrunk and shifted.
   c. The rate of volunteerism has decreased.
4. Decline in religious affiliation

Why these four? For one thing, they surfaced over and over in my research, but my thinking goes beyond that. Ultimately, I prefer to focus on reasons leading to answers that are actionable and can enhance our spiritual growth. Let's consider these four reasons why, as research shows, we have fewer confidants than in the past and why loneliness is so widespread in the world today.

As you consider these, see which category(s) you believe may have influenced your loneliness.

1. *Geographic mobility.* It is no secret that today, more than at any time in human history, people are more able to move from one location to another and are more likely to do so than ever before. "Some experts explain the increase in loneliness by the fact that people are more geographically mobile and therefore are more likely to live apart from friends and family."[22] It used to be far more common for multiple generations of a family to live in the same geographic region. But in today's world, with the ease and affordability of travel, the national or even global nature of various businesses and corporations, and the availability of working off-site, people are on the move like never before. Relocating for the purposes of work or preference is very common, and making multiple moves during our lifetime is not at all unusual. Therefore, not only are relationships often left behind or rendered less intimate because of moving away but people may become more reticent to develop new, deep relationships knowing they won't be living in the same place for long periods of time.

After all, relationships take time to develop and grow, and parting with dear friends can be painful.

2. *Technology.* Entire books are dedicated to this subject, but here I'll offer only a cursory look. Even as technology allows people today to be hyperconnected, it has also created the opportunity to have arm's-length relationships—ones with no true intimacy. The result? Physical connections are increasingly being replaced with digital connections. The risk is that digital connections and social networks "offer the illusion of companionship without the demands of friendship. Our networked life allows us to hide from each other, even as we are tethered to each other."[23] And to make matters worse, "we seek more and more privacy, and feel more and more alienated and lonely when we get it."[24]

Numerous trends indicate we are becoming less socially connected even as our technical connections abound. The world of social media can easily foster expectations to have more "friends" or "followers" so we can keep up with others who have a greater following than we have. This may lead to a longer list of connections on our various social media sites but also merely gives the illusion of greater connectedness—not true companionship.

One study from the University of Pennsylvania found a link between social media use and decreased well-being. Speaking about the study she and her team conducted, psychologist Melissa G. Hunt said, "Here's the bottom line: Using less social media than you normally would leads to significant decreases in both

depression and loneliness."[25] It shouldn't surprise us
that how people use social media has been shown to
determine its influence on their sense of isolation. "If
you're passively using it, if you're just scrolling feeds,
that's associated with more negative effects," she says.
"But if you're using it to reach out and connect to
people to facilitate other kinds of [in-person] interactions, it's associated with more positive effects."[26]

I appreciate this quote from author Brené Brown:
"The way we engage with social media is like fire—
you can use them to keep yourself warm and nourished, or you can burn down the barn."[27]

My own conclusion is that using technology and social media to stay in touch with real friends and loved
ones can be a great thing, but using it as a *substitute*
for real connections is not. But even then, *all things in
moderation*! Why? Because research shows that young
adults with heavy use of social media are at high risk
of experiencing social anxiety and social isolation.[28]

3. *Decrease in common cultural connections.* There has
   been a dramatic decrease and/or change in many of
   the institutions that at one time created our sense
   of community. First and foremost is the change
   in family makeup. Did you know that the second
   most common household type today, worldwide, is
   the single-person household? The most recent US
   census data, for example, show that more than a
   quarter of the population lives alone—the highest
   rate ever recorded. Until the 1960s that was actually
   quite rare. In America the number of single-person
   households has more than doubled, so that today

they outnumber households of married couples with minor children.[29] In fact, more than half of the US population is unmarried, and nearly one-third of those who are married are in a poor relationship.[30] Also, the size, makeup, and availability of community organizations have dramatically shrunk and shifted. Dr. Bianca Suanet of Vrije Universiteit Amsterdam, lead author of the Longitudinal Aging Study Amsterdam (a long-term study of the social, physical, cognitive, and emotional functioning of older adults), made a telling statement: "People must manage their social lives better today than ever before because traditional communities, which provided social outlets, such as neighborhoods, churches and extended families, have lost strength in recent decades."[31] Likewise, Dr. Jennifer Caudle, assistant professor of family medicine at Rowan University School of Osteopathic Medicine, observes that "many of the institutions that once created community, such as schools, churches and neighborhood organizations, have been replaced by online versions or more solitary activities, adding to modern day loneliness."[32]

Related to this shift in community organizations, rates of volunteerism have also decreased, according to research by the University of Maryland's Do Good Institute. Also, an increasing percentage of Americans report no religious affiliation, suggesting declines in the kinds of religious and other institutional connections that can provide community opportunities for volunteerism.

This research quote seems to summarize the issue of the decrease in common cultural connections:

Living alone, being unmarried (single, divorced, widowed), no participation in social groups, fewer friends, and strained relationships are not only all risk factors for premature mortality (Holt-Lunstad et al., 2010), but also increase risk for loneliness. Retirement and physical impairments (e.g., mobility, hearing loss) may also increase risk for social isolation (AARP, n.d.).[33]

Of note, women were more likely than men to report a lack of companionship, researchers have found, and living alone, not working, and living in lower-income homes were all associated with feeling lonely.

4. *Decline in religious affiliation.* Research reveals that there is a significant decline in the number of people who are religiously affiliated. I should let you know that I squirm a bit in using the word *religious*, because when talking about my own faith I don't refer to myself as being religious but rather having a personal relationship with Jesus Christ. But in this context researchers are referring to people of all faiths, and here is what they have discovered: "Religiously affiliated Americans, on average, are as actively devout as they have always been," writes researcher and author Dr. Francie Hart Broghammer. "The number of religiously affiliated individuals, however, is in sharp decline. As of 2014, for every American that adopted a specific religious affiliation, 4.2 Americans did just the opposite, abandoning their formal religious identity."[34]

Think for a moment how that would increase loneliness in our world. Rather than becoming or remaining a part of an active faith community, which includes regular worship together, personally sharing deeply held truths and personal values, and many types of joint activities, week in, week out, year in, year out, vast numbers of people in our culture are abandoning those connections.

Now that you've thought about those four categories, take a look at these answers my surveyed military spouses gave as to why they were lonely. All five of these answers fit into one of the four categories above. Can you spot where they fall? Can you see the cultural factors that have influenced your own loneliness?

- "Distance from my family and lack of close friends."
- "Being far away from my parents and my family."
- "Lack of meaningful relationships."
- "I'm new to the area and it's hard to break into existing groups to meet others."
- "My husband is deployed, so I'm handling life's most intense issues alone."

Are You Isolated?

In chapter 1 we defined the word *isolation* in a negative sense, meaning "keeping apart, separating, withdrawing, and becoming self-focused and self-occupied." It stresses detachment from others and may be voluntary or involuntary.

71

The choice to isolate in this sense—to withdraw from others and turn inward—is a destructive choice. It is dangerous to our mental, physical, spiritual, and relational health.

During the early days of the 2020 COVID-19 pandemic, it was determined that while in lockdown people used their phones for calling one another more. We had been using our phones a lot for texting, email, scrolling, and taking pictures. But during these months people began to call and talk to others—not just text. It seems we wanted a real live person to talk to—a human voice on the other end. Verizon discovered that they were handling 800 million wireless conversational calls a day, which is twice the number of calls on Mother's Day. "When we are in a time of stress, when we are in a time of worry, when we are under pressure, what we need more than anything else is the human voice."[35]

As I write this, we are still in the midst of the pandemic—it has gone on for many months. My governor has seriously restricted us. People are going stir-crazy by having to stay home. We are being told to wear masks and stand at least six to ten feet away from others. No church services. Most businesses are closed. No sitting inside restaurants—only takeout. No gatherings—including family—of more than ten people. When you go to the grocery store, everyone is wearing a mask and there is a sense of gloom. One of my grocery stores restricts the number of shoppers. Life has changed drastically. No one seems to know when our lives will return to normal, and we are not sure it will ever return to what it was before. While we live in isolation, it is lonely.

But when I take my daily walk it has been interesting to see so many neighbors out walking too. We stop and chat for a bit—six to ten feet apart. On a "normal" day, that wouldn't happen. We'd all be scurrying off to some appointment or running an errand, not really taking the time to visit. So in that sense this pause has been good for us.

The earth has been able to rest as well. Quieting down and sheltering in place has its benefits—some measured in unlikely ways. The seismologists even say they can detect a slowing of the earth.

> Global containment measures to combat the spread of the coronavirus have seemingly made the world much quieter. Scientists are noticing it, too. Around the world, seismologists are observing a lot less ambient seismic noise—meaning, the vibrations generated by cars, trains, buses and people going about their daily lives. And in the absence of that noise, Earth's upper crust is moving just a little less. Thomas Lecocq, a geologist and seismologist at the Royal Observatory in Belgium, first pointed out this phenomenon in Brussels. Brussels is seeing about a 30% to 50% reduction in ambient seismic noise since mid-March, around the time the country started implementing school and business closures and other social distancing measures, according to Lecocq. That noise level is on par with what seismologists would see on Christmas Day, he said.[36]

And there is also less pollution. Nitrogen dioxide, a gas spewed by cars, trucks, power plants, and other industrial activity, has been reduced in a marked way.

We tend to balk at loneliness and solitude. But we shouldn't. We need quiet and solitude for our own health. It is a time to settle and grow quiet within ourselves. How else can we hear the "still, small voice"—the whisper of God?

But the downside of all this is isolation. Unhealthy isolation. Typically, prolonged isolation gives way to poor nutrition, lack of interest in things you were interested in before, boredom, and withdrawal. Isolation can lead to feelings of loneliness, cause conflicts with others, render us less able to deal with stressful situations, and cause us to have difficulty making decisions. It can lead to obesity, high blood pressure, heart disease, and a weakened immune system.

According to a meta-analysis co-authored by Julianne Holt-Lunstad, PhD, a professor of psychology and neuroscience at Brigham Young University, lack of social connection heightens health risks as much as smoking 15 cigarettes a day or having alcohol use disorder. She's also found that loneliness and social isolation are twice as harmful to physical and mental health as obesity.[37]

No, prolonged isolation is not healthy. After all, isn't isolation considered to be the worst punishment in our prison system apart from execution? It is not wise for a person to self-isolate, and it is usually a symptom of something else going on. We may be hiding an alcohol or drug problem. We may be full of fear and anxiety. We may be terribly insecure. We may be depressed. And we are not called to isolate ourselves. Scripture says, "He who separates himself seeks his own desire, he quarrels against all sound wisdom" (Prov. 18:1). I know when I was suffering with depression my tendency was to just isolate myself. I didn't want to see people. I didn't have the energy to go out. I just stayed at home, isolated. That was not good for me. I need people—we all do. It's the way we were created.

Scripture tells us to "consider how to stimulate one another to love and good deeds, not forsaking our own assembling together, as is the habit of some, but encouraging one another" (Heb. 10:24–25). I have always loved Christian fellowship—gathering over a potluck dinner or luncheon with those who create in me a desire for a deeper walk with Christ. I like to discuss ideas and books of all sorts. I like to be challenged in my thinking. And I am happy "to agree to disagree." I like a lively discussion. And it doesn't always have to be a gathering of Christians. I have friends from all walks of life. I enjoy their perspectives.

During the pandemic, I have enjoyed a three-times-a-week group phone call with friends. All of us have been "locked down," but now two who live in another state are enjoying a bit more freedom. They report to us how "normalcy" is faring in their state. We have talked issues, politics, faith, church, family, books, podcasts . . . you name it, we have covered it. It has been a lifeline for me—and I think for all of us.

I remember the first time I had to go to a function by myself after my divorce. I was anxious. I felt that walking by myself into the room full of people would scream, "She's alone!" What would people think? But I knew I had to overcome that feeling. It required a lot of energy, but I took the first step, then the second step. And this is how we overcome those things that keep us bound in isolation—step by step. It isn't easy. Isolation can be our comfort zone. It's where we feel secure. We don't always want to break free, but we must.

What Does Your Faith Have to Do with Loneliness?

The "horizontal" component of faith ties us to a real-life, hold-hands-and-pray-together community. This community is rich with cradle-to-grave relationships founded on a shared biblical appreciation of human nature and its flaws and the importance of forgiveness.[38]

Why does having faith seem to have an impact on loneliness? Here is one quote that sheds some light on that question:

A new study . . . finds that a combination of religious involvement, family life, and geographic stability tend to be the best preventive measures for loneliness—commitments that the younger generation lacks.[39]

And another:

Americans in general who are members of religious congregations are less likely to feel lonely. The study finds that 45 percent of Americans who do not belong to a congregation feel lonely at least once in a while compared to 35 percent of those who belong to a church or other house of worship.[40]

On that same topic of religion and loneliness, according to writer Dennis Prager,

And now we come to the biggest problem of all: the lack of meaning. . . . And nothing has given Americans—or any other people, for that matter—as much meaning as religion. But since World War II, God and religion have been relegated to the dustbin of history. The result? More than a third of

Americans born after 1980 affiliate with no religion. This is
unprecedented in American history; until this generation,
the vast majority of Americans have been religious. Maybe,
just maybe, the decline of religion—the greatest provider of
meaning, while certainly not the only—is the single biggest
factor in the increasing sadness and loneliness among Americans (and so many others). A 2016 study published in the
American Medical Association JAMA Psychiatry journal
found that American women who attended a religious service at least once a week were five times less likely to commit
suicide. Common sense suggests the same is probably true
of men.[41]

Of course, this "mystery" about the link between declining religious practice and loneliness is not a mystery at all
to those of us who understand we were designed first and
foremost to be in relationship with God and then with one
another. I now see the words of Jesus in Matthew 23:37
in a whole new light: "Jerusalem, Jerusalem, who kills the
prophets and stones those who are sent to her! How often
I wanted to gather your children together, the way a hen
gathers her chicks under her wings."

Consider the great compassion and love Jesus has for all the
lonely people, including us. May we, too, have such compassion
on all those working so hard to keep their loneliness a secret.

Marcus's Story

I am well aware of how temporary my own experiences of
loneliness have been compared to the lengthy ordeals so
many other people have faced or are facing now. Take for
example Marcus, who is incarcerated in prison. I met Marcus

when I visited his prison, and he recently sent me a letter. I share it with you with his kind permission.

I have been in prison for over fifteen years and have found loneliness to be overwhelmingly present in my life. For those of us who are serving long amounts of time behind bars, we find that our pre-prison relationships (wives, friends, and even very close family) begin to fade and dissipate. When this happens, I find myself yearning for love and affirmations that prove that I matter to someone . . . anyone. Loneliness has affected me in a myriad of ways over the years. I found that my self-worth began to come into question. I began to tell myself that I did not matter and my family and friends were right in their decision to remove themselves from my life. Loneliness allowed me to trust less and to guard myself more. I began to isolate and retreat emotionally from feeling or showing love and compassion toward others who were directly in my life. . . .

I physically gained weight and began to self-medicate. Loneliness fueled a desire to fill the gap that love and meaningful relationships once had occupied. . . . I spiraled in my addiction to ease the pain that loneliness caused. Loneliness seemed to exacerbate the pain of lost friendships . . . and kept me painfully aware of the wounds that I had caused.

Having said these things about loneliness over the years, I found that I was missing something through all those moments . . . Christ! When I accepted that Christ needs to be my hope, my loneliness became less and less. Now I'm not saying that all of my lone-liness feelings have vanished, but they are not nearly as heavy. Through Jesus, I have found that when I look to other people to feel accepted and give me self-worth, I will always come up short. And something has happened since relying on Christ. Many of my relationships from my pre-incarceration days have been restored and amends have been made. God is good!

It sounds like Marcus has figured out what faith has to do with loneliness. This quote seems to have been written to describe his journey:

Faith does not promise a life free from suffering. Instead, it offers purpose in and guidance through suffering. Religious faith can instill a sense of meaning and purpose that transcends the present struggle; it allows people to survive anguish and find meaning in suffering.[42]

We started this chapter with some good news, and we'll end it with some good news as well. If you've been carrying the well-kept secret of your own loneliness, I hope God is beginning to shed some light on it for you. In the next chapter we'll bring God's light into the dark side of loneliness.

In him was life, and that life was the light of all mankind. The light shines in the darkness, and the darkness has not overcome it.

John 1:4–5

5

The Dark Side of Loneliness

Chronic loneliness not only makes us miserable, then, it can also make us sick.

John T. Cacioppo and William Patrick[1]

I cannot imagine a lonelier, more desperate situation than being in the belly of a great fish. Knowing my plan had been to get away from God, I'd worry I may have actually succeeded in doing just that. I wonder if that's what went through Jonah's mind as he was tossed around with the other contents of the fish's belly.

Some doubt Jonah's story is true. But Jesus referred to Jonah as a real person who was in the belly of a sea monster for three days (Matt. 12:39–41), so I take the story as an historical account of what happened. In that spirit, and with some creative license, I want to retell the story here.

> It was dark. Smelly. Damp. Scary. Jonah had no clue what else was sloshing around in there with him. *Yuck!* He had to admit he'd done it to himself. He had blatantly disobeyed God by running away.

God had given him a mission to go to Nineveh to "cry against it, for their wickedness has come up before Me" (Jonah 1:2), and Jonah didn't like that one bit. Perhaps he was frightened, as the Assyrians who inhabited Nineveh were known as being a violent, cruel, and ruthless people. Or perhaps he just didn't want to give God's message to these wicked people—the sworn enemies of Israel. Whatever his reason, instead of obeying he decided he'd run as far away from Nineveh as he could. He got on a boat sailing for Tarshish, a city that was over three thousand miles in the opposite direction, and then settled below deck for a nap. Jonah didn't seem the least bit nervous about running from God, for he fell into such a deep sleep he had no idea what pure chaos was going on topside. The Lord had created a strong wind, and the storm was so violent the ship was about to break up.

The next thing he knew, the captain was shaking him awake, shouting at him to pray to his God since all the other crew members were praying to theirs—to no avail.

The boat was pitching and rolling, riding up one giant wave and sliding down another. Rogue waves were crashing into it, terrifying the seasoned sailors. They drew lots to see who was causing this unprecedented storm. After the lot fell on Jonah, the crew peppered him with questions. "Who are you?" "Where are you going?" "What are you doing?" And the biggest, "On whose account has this calamity struck us?" (1:8).

Jonah admitted the truth. He was a Hebrew, and he feared the God who made heaven and earth—but he hadn't feared Him enough to obey Him. When they discovered Jonah was fleeing from his God, they became even more frightened than they had been before. "How could you do this?" they asked him.

As the sea grew even more violent, Jonah told them to throw him into the sea. These good men refused and tried to row to shore. They didn't want to see him die, even though he had put them in such grave danger. However, the storm was too much for them.

They prayed to God and asked that they not be blamed or die because they did what Jonah recommended. Then they picked him up and threw him overboard. The seas immediately calmed. Moments later, along came a great big fish that scooped up Jonah and swallowed him whole.

Jonah was now alone. Running from God will do that to you.

Was it at this moment that he wondered if he'd actually succeeded in his goal to run from God? I can imagine he became desperate. Surely it was like being in hell—or what he imagined hell to be. Except this place wasn't hot; instead, he was enveloped in a sort of sickening mugginess. No fresh air. Just horrible smells and slimy things and gurgling noises. It had to have been revolting.

For three days, Jonah rolled around in that slime and stench, fearing for his life. Then he prayed—a desperate crying out to the Lord. "I called out of my distress to the LORD, and He answered me" (2:2). What an act of mercy that God answered him and ordered the fish to spit him out onto dry land.

Sucking in fresh air, Jonah was overcome with relief and overjoyed at his freedom. But he was a sight to behold. His skin was all shriveled and white. And oh, the stench!

Then God gave him a second chance to obey. He repeated His command to preach repentance to the city of Nineveh. This time, without hesitation, Jonah took off for Nineveh, alone, a 750-mile journey from his original starting place.

His first day in the great city, he cried out the words God had given him to say: the city, the people, needed to repent or God was going to destroy them for their wickedness.

Jonah wasn't the least prepared for what happened next. This terribly wicked city repented—from the king on down to the people in the streets.

Jonah, rather than rejoicing over their repentance, was furious. He didn't want these people to know God's grace and goodness. He wanted God to destroy these wicked enemies of Israel. He got so angry with God that he became depressed and asked God to let him die.

Jonah went back to dwelling in his own negative mindset, not looking at the situation from God's perspective. His thoughts churned with anger, resentment, and despair. He continued those destructive thought patterns uninterrupted. He didn't call out to God for insight or help or forgiveness for his own attitudes. He just grumbled about God forgiving those vile Ninevites. Now he was stewing again—not in the juices of the belly of a fish this time but in his own caustic juices, marinating in them. He was all by himself and throwing a big pity party complete with party balloons and confetti.

Soon God interrupted Jonah's self-pity. "The LORD said, 'Do you have good reason to be angry?'" (4:4).

Jonah didn't even answer. He sulked and skulked outside the city and made a shelter for himself from where he could watch what might happen to Nineveh. Oh, how he hoped God would still see fit to destroy it like He had Sodom and Gomorrah.

God caused a plant to quickly grow up around Jonah, which provided great shade from the desert heat, and he was glad for it. But the next morning God caused a worm to gnaw on the plant and make it wither. The sun beat down on Jonah and a scorching east wind blew. Now he was really mad!

God asked him again if he had a good reason to be angry. Like a toddler, Jonah crossed his arms, pouted, and told God he had every right to be angry.

Then came God's teaching moment: if Jonah had concern for a plant that he did not plant nor have anything to do with its growth, why couldn't he have compassion on a city as large as Nineveh, full of people God created and loved?

Jonah, from our perspective (and God's), really had no right to be angry about a withered plant, nor about how God chose to handle a nation's repentance, and he had allowed a different type of plant to grow up in him, one he did tend and water: the plant of anger.

Which Direction Shall We Run?

I love that story because we are all like Jonah! We don't like to obey God when it's uncomfortable. Then when we get in trouble we holler for God. I also love the fact that we know the story because Jonah told on himself!

What is your attitude about your loneliness? Are you frustrated and angry that you feel lonely? At who? At God for placing you in these circumstances? At others for not reaching out to you? At yourself for not handling relationships differently? Are you despairing—feeling hopeless—about the possibilities of seeing your loneliness transformed? Are you afraid you will always feel this way?

Proverbs 16:25 tells us that "there is a way which seems right to a man, but its end is the way of death." Jonah found that out the hard way when he ran away from God. By God's mercy, he didn't die in the ocean, though being swallowed by a fish must have been a harrowing experience. But Jonah didn't run *toward* God. *He turned inward.* He isolated himself. He took a seat on the side of a mountain and pouted rather than embracing what God was up to.

Jonah is a good example of how anger and despair can distort our thinking. He had shut God out and lost any sensitivity to Him. A dangerous place to be.

Since Jonah told the story on himself, I have to believe God's grace touched his heart in a profound way and he found his way back to humility and obedience. And so he told his story for others to learn to obey God and rejoice in His compassion.

Jonah's story raises an important question for you and me to consider. In the midst of our loneliness, what direction shall we run? Toward God or away from Him? Upward or inward?

I know. I made this mistake myself. And it could have cost me my life.

I tell this story in greater detail in my book *In Every Pew Sits a Broken Heart*, but here I'll quickly give just a few of the details so you understand my point. I'd been married for eighteen years when I learned that my husband, the father of my children, had been unfaithful to me a number of times over several years. Though deeply hurt, I suggested we seek counseling together but tell no one—which we did for about a year and a half before I reached the painful, heartbreaking decision to seek divorce. It was a difficult time, to say the least, made all the more painful by the fact that many who did not know the full story were admonishing me to reconcile rather than divorce. They, of course, hadn't been part of my long journey to reconcile and heal the relationship and save the marriage, but the pressure and disapproval I felt from them was crushing.

One Sunday during this time my pastor preached a rich message that stirred all those dark, negative feelings in me and brought all that conflict to the surface. In my book, I wrote,

> For perhaps the only time in my life, I felt separated from God in an ultimate sense. . . . I thought God had rejected me and was no longer on my side. At that moment, I was blind to all but my pain and what appeared an endless struggle. I despaired. I ran from the church when the service was over.
>
> Shaking, I drove myself home, parked the car in the driveway, and went straight for my bathroom, looking for razor blades. I anxiously searched my bathroom drawers, then my husband's drawers, fumbling with the items and products. Thoughts of the children passed through my mind. I knew they depended on me and would be deeply affected by a suicide, but I was in such pain. I was blinded by pain. I kept looking and looking, but there were no razor blades anywhere. None. Anywhere. I finally gave up and sank into a chair. I took a deep breath.

Until now, I've never fully understood the impact of the next five words in my account, but they are powerful: "Then a friend came by."

My story goes on.

> Thankfully, my friend came over to check on me and helped bring me back to center, at least in that moment. The corrective influence a loving person can have on our distorted perception of reality is very great. We need people. Never underestimate the healing that God can administer through a friend.[2]

Yes! Exactly! Let us never underestimate God's power sent through a friend. Loneliness left unchecked can be very destructive, so always remember the wisdom of Ecclesiastes 4:9–12.

> Two are better than one because they have a good return for their labor; for if either of them falls, the one will lift up his companion. But woe to the one who falls when there is not another to lift him up! Furthermore, if two lie down together they keep warm, but how can one be warm alone? And if one can overpower him who is alone, two can resist him. A cord of three strands is not quickly torn apart.

How grateful I am that in my desperate situation I didn't even have to call a friend. God sent one to my door! And in the company and caring of my friend, my despair lifted. My sadness wasn't gone, but my reason was restored.

The Heartbreaking Damages of Loneliness

I came across a term during my research that caused my heart to ache as it brought to mind the harrowing memory of my frantic search for razor blades to end my life: "Deaths of Despair." I'll let the research speak for itself.

> Economically, America is more prosperous than it has ever been. We are richer, more connected . . . and have more information available to us than ever before. And yet, we are in the midst of a crisis that is claiming thousands of American lives: loneliness. . . .
> Since the turn of the century, Americans have been dying from suicide, alcohol-related illnesses, and drug overdoses

at a rate that has never before been seen. Princeton econo-
mists Anne Case and Angus Deaton have aptly named these
tragedies "Deaths of Despair." In fact, suicide is now the
second leading cause of death for American teenagers and
the tenth leading cause of death for Americans, overall. The
suicide rate has increased more than 30 percent in half of
U.S. states since 1999. Equally harrowing, drug overdose
is the leading cause of death for Americans under the age
of fifty.[3]

Is loneliness really so serious? YES! Is it deadly? Absolutely! In more ways than one. Loneliness is fraught with
dangers to our physical, mental, and emotional health.

Since we are on the subject of suicide, let's begin with a
look at the danger loneliness poses to our mental health.
I could fill a few pages with nothing but quotes from researchers on this subject, but I will spare you. I've chosen
this next quote to get us started because it goes to the
heart, from a scientific point of view, of how absolutely essential the need for a sense of "belonging" is to the human
psyche.

According to Abraham Maslow's hierarchy of needs, after
basic physiologic and safety requirements have been met
(i.e., food and shelter), the next greatest human need is social
connectedness: to feel that we belong. Without this, Maslow
postulated that humans could not successfully pursue higher
aspirations such as growth, autonomy, and self-actualization.
The death toll that has resulted from America's lack of connection certainly seems to give credence to Maslow's theory.
It also suggests that to return to a state of health and prosperity, we must solve the problem of loneliness.[4]

Is it any wonder, then, that loneliness can augment depression and anxiety and even increase a person's risk of dementia? We've all heard of the research about infants in orphanages who suffer from "failure to thrive."

> Failure to thrive is a medical condition where an infant/child fails to grow or gain weight appropriately over a consistent period of time. In orphanages, the number one cause of failure to thrive is simply a lack of touch, stimulation and love. A child may even die due to missing these essential requirements for growth. . . . Touching, holding and talking to an infant are required for proper stimulation. Without this stimulation, the child loses the motivation to eat and brain development is delayed. This is similar to a deep depression in that the baby seems to give up on living.[5]

Just as the need for touch is true of infants, it is true of all humans of all ages. Our social relationships are widely considered crucial to our emotional well-being, but they may also be a *biological* need, touch being vital to physical well-being and even survival. Social isolation is so distressing that solitary confinement has long been used as a form of punishment and even torture.

You will recall my references in earlier chapters to Vivek Murthy, the former US surgeon general. He writes,

> During my years caring for patients, the most common pathology I saw was not heart disease or diabetes; it was loneliness. . . . I found that loneliness was often in the background of clinical illness, contributing to disease and making it harder for patients to cope and heal. . . . Loneliness is also associated with a greater risk of cardiovascular disease,

dementia, depression, and anxiety. At work, loneliness reduces task performance, limits creativity, and impairs other aspects of executive function such as reasoning and decision making.[6]

Murthy also explains,

Loneliness causes stress, and long-term or chronic stress leads to more frequent elevations of a key stress hormone, cortisol. It is also linked to higher levels of inflammation in the body. This in turn damages blood vessels and other tissues, increasing the risk of heart disease, diabetes, joint disease, depression, obesity, and premature death. Chronic stress can also hijack your brain's pre-frontal cortex, which governs decision making, planning, emotional regulation, analysis, and abstract thinking.[7]

As I began to absorb all this discouraging news, my comprehension of the seriousness of loneliness leaped to an entirely new level. Loneliness is about far more than "feeling sad" over a lack of connection. God created us to be in intimate connection with Him and others, so loneliness is an attack on our bodies that threatens our very survival. No wonder it can make us feel so desperate emotionally. This emotional pain of loneliness is a God-given alarm system that something needs to change—and fast!

For many years it's been well known and accepted that loneliness can lead to psychiatric disorders such as anxiety, depression, and schizophrenia. But only in recent years have we come to realize how destructive it can be to the body as well. In 2015 analysts pooled research data from seventy unique studies that followed 3.4 million people over a period of seven years. The startling results? Lonely people had a risk of dying that was 26 percent higher than the average population. That number rose to 32 percent if they lived alone.[8]

Dr. Steve Cole, an NIH-funded researcher who studies loneliness at the University of California, Los Angeles, says this: "Lonely people have differences in their biology that make them more vulnerable to disease." Dr. Cole has studied how loneliness affects the immune system. That research indicates "loneliness may alter the tendency of cells in the immune system to promote inflammation. Inflammation is necessary to help our bodies heal from injury. But when it goes on too long, it may raise the risk of chronic diseases."[9]

Dramatically dealing with our loneliness isn't just a nice feel-good idea so we don't "feel sad." This is a "must-do" so we might live healthy lives! It is imperative we tackle the issue of our loneliness so we might thrive as God intended us to thrive, deeply connected to Him and to others. Do you remember in chapter 3 we discussed that God made us in His image, designing us for community? Now we see how that design goes from the cellular level all the way through the psychological level. Our *whole* being is designed for connection to others, and when loneliness attacks it attacks us at every level.

According to *Psychology Today*, "Loneliness makes our bodies feel like they're under attack. Loneliness causes an immediate and severe bodily reaction."[10] This isn't just true of "some" people. It is true of all people of every race.

An extensive study found that social isolation increases the risk of premature death from every cause for every race (*American Journal of Epidemiology*, vol. 188, no. 1, 2019) . . . among black participants, social isolation doubled the risk of early death, while it increased the risk among white participants by 60 to 84 percent.[11]

This next quote is not only true but poignant. "Loneliness is associated with higher blood pressure and heart disease—it literally breaks our hearts."[12]

Did you catch that? Loneliness *literally breaks our hearts.*

Putting all this together, loneliness can result in multiple long-term health problems. It can affect our immune systems, increase our risk of premature death, elevate our stress responses, augment depression and anxiety, lead to a greater risk of cardiovascular disease and dementia, reduce our task performance, limit our creativity, and impair other aspects of executive function such as reasoning and decision-making.

Does that sound overwhelming? Yes! But do not despair! Despair does us no favors and only drives an even greater wedge between us and the living God who cherishes us.

God Transforms Bitter to Sweet

If we want a powerful picture of the consequences of despair we need look no further than four verses, Exodus 15:22–25. God had just delivered the Hebrew nation from the clutches of the Egyptian army. They had just crossed through the Red Sea on dry land and were now safely on the other side, their pursuers buried in the sea. The people rejoiced, singing a song of joy and victory:

> I will sing to the LORD, for He is highly exalted;
> The horse and its rider He has hurled into the sea.
> The LORD is my strength and song,

And He has become my salvation;
This is my God, and I will praise Him;
My father's God, and I will extol Him.
The LORD is a warrior;
The LORD is His name.
Pharaoh's chariots and his army He has cast into the
  sea;
And the choicest of his officers are drowned in the
  Red Sea. (Exod. 15:1–4)

This song of praise for deliverance continues for another fourteen verses. The people praised God for all they could think of, from the wind to the fear instilled in their enemies by such a great act of redemption. They were thrilled and excited. Moses's sister, Miriam, led a chorus of praise to God. They had been delivered. What a wonderful day it was!

From the banks of the Red Sea, Moses led them for three days into the wilderness of Shur—a barren, dry, unfriendly place. Add several million people to the mix and the situation got ugly pretty quickly. By now their water bags were empty. Their jugs were dry. And they couldn't find any water.

They came to a place called Marah, saw water, and were thrilled. I can just see them running into the water, splashing, feeling relieved. But it soon came to a disappointing end. The water was bitter and undrinkable. When you are desperately thirsty, you will drink just about anything, so it must have been bad. Not only were they thirsty but their herds were suffering. They needed water—soon.

They turned on Moses just as they had on the other side of the Red Sea when they thought they were going to be overrun by the Egyptians. The wonderful praises they had sung three days before were now turned to grumbling. Had they so soon forgotten God's mighty power to deliver them? It was all Moses's fault, they complained. After all, he had encouraged them to leave Egypt, and now they were in this godforsaken wilderness and they and their flocks were going to die of thirst without water. How lonely Moses must have felt in his leadership of these people.

But in his loneliness, Moses turned toward God, unlike Jonah, who turned away. The Scripture says he "cried out to the LORD" (v. 25). I doubt he used pretty, theological words in his prayer. I think Moses, who was frustrated with these people and probably tired and thirsty himself, cried out for help from the God who had so marvelously delivered them out of the hands of the Egyptians. Moses knew God could and would deliver again. He had a dependable track record, so Moses cried out to Him not in despair but for help.

In answer to Moses's prayer God showed him a tree. Not exactly the kind of answer I would have expected! But Moses knew what to do with it. He threw it into the waters and they became sweet. The people satiated their thirst and filled their water bags and jars. They then journeyed on and came to a place of twelve springs with an abundance of water.

When we cry out in our loneliness for help, God shows us a tree—the cross. As we trust the One who died for us on that tree, we find Living Water and our thirst is quenched. Jesus promised, "If anyone is thirsty, let him come to Me and drink. He who believes in Me, as the Scripture said, 'From his innermost being will flow rivers of living water'" (John 7:37–38). As we thirst for companionship, connection, and belonging, may we, too, turn to Jesus to have our thirst quenched.

Instead of despairing over the very dangerous consequences of loneliness, we can focus our attention on 2 Corinthians 4, verses 8–9 and 16:

> We are afflicted in every way, but not crushed; perplexed, but not despairing; persecuted, but not forsaken; struck down, but not destroyed. . . . Therefore we do not lose heart, but though our outer man is decaying, yet our inner man is being renewed day by day.

We can all take great hope in the truth that, through Jesus Christ, we are being transformed day by day!

We've seen the bad news in this chapter about the dark side of loneliness: lacking social connection significantly increases our risk for premature mortality and a poorer quality of life. Now for the good news! The opposite is also true. Becoming more socially connected—to God and to others—significantly reduces those risks. We'll explore ways to put this good news into action in the chapters ahead.

Therefore we do not lose heart.
2 Corinthians 4:16

6

The Transformation of Loneliness

It is possible both to accept and to endure loneliness without bitterness when there is a vision of glory beyond.

Elisabeth Elliot[1]

A caterpillar becomes a butterfly. An acorn becomes an oak tree. Dusk becomes night. Dawn becomes day. *Transformation*: "a dramatic and thorough change in form or appearance."[2] Such transformations seem miraculous, don't they? They occur as an act of God, without human intervention.

Then there are transformations that require human effort. A weed patch becomes a garden. A stack of lumber becomes a shed. A clump of clay becomes a flowerpot. All stunning transformations where the end result bears little resemblance, if any, to the original materials.

What will your loneliness become?

I believe this is an important question to consider. Your loneliness could become bitterness or depression, withdrawal or isolation—or it might become motivation or purpose, an impetus to change. I believe that if we work in partnership with God, loneliness can become a pathway to a deeper relationship with Him and others. That's why I chose my favorite loneliness quote from Elisabeth Elliot as the epigraph for this book: "Loneliness is a wilderness, but through receiving it as a gift, accepting it from the hand of God, and offering it back to Him with thanksgiving, it may become a pathway to holiness, to glory, and to God Himself."[3]

The Little Girl Who Became a Poet

Jane Hess Merchant was born into a Tennessee farm family in 1919. As a toddler, she broke one of her legs. Not long after that leg healed, her other leg broke. She was diagnosed with osteogenesis imperfecta, or brittle bone disease. Her case became so severe that at the age of twelve both of her legs and one arm were broken simply by moving her from her bed to a wheelchair. From that tender age she spent the rest of her life bedridden. Imagine the loneliness she must have endured.

She'd always been an avid reader, but once confined to bed she also began to write poetry. At the age of twenty-one Jane also became deaf as a side effect of the disease. An even greater loneliness and sense of isolation descended upon her. This sent her spiraling into depression, during which time she quit writing poetry and corresponding with friends. Then she read a book by Harry Emerson Fosdick that declared that one's responses to circumstances, rather than circumstances themselves, determine the quality of one's life. He used the examples of the deaf composer Beethoven and the blind and deaf Helen Keller to make his point.

Jane was inspired and so began her journey out of loneliness and depression into a dedicated life of reading and writing.

Jane wrote, "I rely on Fosdick saying, 'We all have cellars in our houses, but we don't have to live in them.'"⁴ (I love that!) Eventually, at the age of twenty-seven, Jane mustered the courage to seek publication of her poems. Her work subsequently appeared in a number of magazines, including *Good Housekeeping* and *The Saturday Evening Post*. She published her first book of poems in 1956 at the age of thirty-seven. When she died at the age of fifty-two, she'd had 2,080 poems and two books published.

In 1989 my mother wrote the foreword for *The Life and Poetry of Jane Hess Merchant: A Window to Eternity* by Sarah Jorunn Oftedal Rickets. What a delight it would be for me to be able to discuss Jane's work with Mother now. Mother, too, was a poet. In the preface to her first book of poetry, *Sitting by My Laughing Fire*, she wrote, "I wrote because I had to. It was write or develop an ulcer—or forget. I chose to write. At times I wrote for the sheer fun."⁵ And the world is richer for it.

A Partnership with God

It often surprises people to learn that my mother lived a lonely life. Oh, she had people around her, but she never felt she could confide in anyone. Her life was lived under a microscope. After all, she was married to one of the world's most famous men. How does one live in his shadow without feeling left out? You can only sing "Wind Beneath My Wings" so many times! But Mother would say that it really didn't take anything special—that it all boiled down to choices. Life is made up of choices. Good ones. Bad ones. Ones we wish we could get a "do-over" for and make again. Choices we'd like to forget. Choices we can relish. And she made a lifetime of wise choices.

My mother was born in China during the time of warlords and bandits. She grew up hearing gunfire in the distance at night and seeing the bombs in their racks as Japanese war planes swooped low over their compound. But she didn't remember fear being part of her childhood. She lived the statement, "Fear not tomorrow, God is already there."

My mother's father, Nelson Bell, was a busy missionary surgeon who became chief of staff of one of the world's largest Presbyterian hospitals at the time in Tsingkiangpu, China, now named Huai'an. Still, he created a secure, loving home filled with music, quality family experiences, and lots of humor. His fidelity to Christ and His service never wavered, as it was his life's motivation. He adored his wife, Virginia Bell, who had been his childhood sweetheart. She was very talented and creative in her homemaking skills and was a single-mindedly supportive wife. My mother's overwhelming memory of her was the effort she made to keep their home running smoothly and to create a happy environment for the family.

Because Mother grew up in China, she was sent away to boarding school when she reached age thirteen. This was quite typical of missionaries' children in that time. The night before she left, she prayed that God would let her die before morning! But the next morning, off she went, torn from her secure and happy home. What she had witnessed in her family home, she now had to practice for herself: dependence on

God in every circumstance, love for His Word, concern for others above self, and an indomitable spirit displayed with a smile. How did she do it? What was Mother's choice? Early in her life she chose Christ as her home.

When I was a child, life was not easy for Mother with five children to raise, a home to run, a husband rarely home and usually far away, and the world watching for any flaws and expecting her to be perfect. She experienced her share of sorrows, burdens, injustice, confusion, pressure, and hurt. However, I would not say that I ever saw Mother display anger or doubt.

With the heavy responsibility of family, bills to pay, and not enough money to meet the demands, being expected to act and dress appropriately for a position she was never trained for, and a husband who was married to his ministry and often preoccupied, how did she maintain her perspective? What was Mother's choice? Early on she chose Christ as her partner.

Yes, she was lonely without Daddy around, but she didn't let it cripple her. She used those times to reach out to others either through my father and his ministry or through her own ministry to us children, her neighbors, and anyone who came across her path who needed her. Even now, I meet people from all over the country who were in her Sunday school class back in the seventies. They tell me how real she was, how down to earth, how practical in her faith, showing her love and concern for them as people. What was Mother's choice? Early in life she chose the gospel as her purpose.

I cannot recall what my earliest memory of my mother is, but I am quite certain it is associated with joy. Mother chose joy. Joy wasn't automatic or a given. It was a choice, so her one overarching trait was joy. Her joy was all the more notable because her life was not easy. I now understand that such joy did not stem from perfect or ideal circumstances but from a deep, abiding love affair with the Lord Jesus. For early on she chose Christ as her center.

Mother chose to see blessing and joy in everything. Even in her elder years, struck with debilitating arthritis and severe macular degeneration, in that new kind of loneliness and pain she was a light for her family. What was Mother's choice? She chose Christ as her example and so reflected His light throughout her life.

The simple truth is that Mother glorified God by inviting Him, through her choices, to transform her loneliness into purpose. She didn't fight against it but instead offered it to God. She accepted it and saw it as part of God's plan in her life. She accepted that she would be alone rearing five kids. (Of course, with five kids you're not alone very often, but you can be lonely!) Her life, faith, poetry, joy, and choices inspire me to turn eagerly to God to transform my own loneliness from a sad, unfulfilled longing into a "pathway" to God's purposes for me.

Out of the Cellar

When I left home at age thirteen for boarding school in Florida, I was miserably homesick. I made every effort to let Mother know how unhappy I was and how much I wanted to come home. Her well-worn advice, no doubt gleaned from her own memories of being homesick at boarding school in her youth, was for me to look around to find someone who was more homesick than me and cheer them up. It wasn't long before I made new friends and was thoroughly enjoying my first school year there, and then the second year. I loved it. It was a Christian environment in which I felt comfortable. I belonged. But then, when I was fifteen, for reasons I didn't fully understand, Mother and Daddy transferred me to a new boarding school in New York.

I was heartbroken at leaving my friends in Florida. To make matters worse, I had a bad case of mononucleosis, so immediately upon arrival at my new school I had to be isolated in the infirmary. And then Mother left. Talk about feeling alone! When I was finally out of the infirmary I quickly discovered I was a fish out of water. These girls were New York society girls bred in a culture totally foreign to me, and they seemed rough by any standards I had known. I'd never heard four-letter words in my life, and suddenly I was hearing them all around me. I felt intimidated. I think the faculty were believers, but they didn't know quite what to do with me. I didn't know what to do with me!

I had visited my previous school in Florida a number of times because my older sisters, Gigi and Anne, were attending there. So when I moved in as a ninth grader I already knew some people, and one of my friends was there as well. But my parents and I had never even visited the New York school.

I was fifteen and had never in my life known such a season of intense loneliness. I was miserable. Oh, how I wept. And I sent heartsick letters to Mother. My emotional pain was consuming me and I wanted *out*. But I didn't get out. And I didn't understand why God was allowing it. I had no choice but to get through it.

I didn't recognize it at the time, of course, but a transformation was taking place. I look back now and see the gift of spiritual growth my loneliness brought. This intense loneliness thrust me into a relationship with the Lord that was no longer my parents'. I had to find a way to depend upon God for myself. I could turn toward Him or toward something else, but I chose to reach for Him.

Because I was so lonely, I kept my Bible open on my desk and would refer to it during the day just for comfort. Early in the morning I would wake up and hear a rooster crow in the distance and think, *Oh no, another day has started*. And then I would go to my Bible and find strength. My prayer life, though filled with desperation, had probably never been so vibrant. In those choices—turning to God, His Word, and prayer—I was learning to partner with God to transform my loneliness.

Then finally, I made a friend. She was a Christian, and we shared the same values. We bonded and decided to switch out roommates so we could room together. I also discovered that our housemother, a dear woman from England, was also a believer. I have no doubt that God showed me the faith of these two so I'd see His presence around me. The body of Christ was at work. I began to climb out of the cellar I'd been living in. God had me enduring temporary loneliness for His eternal purposes.

Shored up by a newfound confidence, I began to stretch my wings and made an effort to relate more to the other girls. In fact, I became the class president! What a leap from my earliest days as the lonely new girl.

Loneliness, you see, can be a gift. The pain of loneliness is a powerful motivator. "Negative emotions like loneliness, envy, and guilt have an important role to play in a happy life; they're big, flashing signs that something needs to change," says podcaster and author Gretchen Rubin.[6] In my case something did have to change—me! I had to grow into my own faith, my own dependence on God and His Word. Loneliness, when we turn to God as our partner through it, can be a pathway to His purpose for us.

Of course, I had a choice. I could have become angry and bitter at my parents and at God. But that is not what my mother had done. In the face of her trials and loneliness Mother chose Christ as her home, her partner, her center, and her example, and she chose the gospel as her purpose. How grateful I am that I had godly parents who modeled for me what it was to turn toward God in tough times rather than away from Him.

We understand *who* we need to turn to for our transformation: God. Now let's consider a few examples from Scripture of *what* God might transform our loneliness into. As you read these three examples, be thinking of your own loneliness and how God might transform it.

The Man Whose Loneliness Was Transformed into Persistence

Noah and his family lived in a very secular and wicked society, yet in the midst of that, Scripture tells us "Noah was a righteous man, blameless in his time; Noah walked with God" (Gen. 6:9). To be blameless means a person has integrity in all they do, no cutting corners. It must have been very hard to live righteously when the culture around him was so vile. He had no "comfort zone." He never could just be "one of the guys." Was he mocked? Was he tempted to compromise? Were his kids made fun of? Did his kids resent that they were so different from the other kids in the village? Was it a source of tension in his home? We can only imagine.

Not only was he very different from those surrounding him but then God asked him to do something far beyond the norm. God told him to build a ship—a very big ship. We presume this took place in the land we now know as modern-day Iraq. Iraq is desert. Not really near a large body of water suited to an oceangoing vessel. Why did God need a ship? Scripture tells us that God saw the wickedness taking place on earth and was "grieved in His heart. The LORD said, 'I will blot out man whom I have created from the face of the land, from man to animals to creeping things and to birds of the sky; for I am sorry that I have made them'" (vv. 6–7). "Then God said to Noah, 'The end of all flesh has come before Me; for the earth is filled with violence because of them; and behold, I am about to destroy them with the earth. Make for yourself an ark of gopher wood'" (vv. 13–14).

So we have this one righteous man in a sea of wickedness. For six hundred years, he lived with integrity. While in the book of Genesis there is no record of Noah speaking to the people before the flood, 2 Peter 2:5 tells us he was "a preacher of righteousness." He was a lone man preaching and living righteousness in a world that did not want to hear. That is a lonely road. Now in addition to that he had to build this big ship when even rain was scarce! No doubt his contemporaries thought him "odd" to say the least. Crazy is more like it. Did they threaten to lock him up? Did they mock him and jeer at him as he labored? No doubt.

Put yourself in Noah's position. Would you doubt God? Would you wonder if what you'd heard was really what God said? Would you doubt yourself? Would you ask yourself,

Was it my imagination? Who could you talk to? Who would understand you? Would your spouse and family? After a while they may have doubted him or questioned his sanity along with everyone else.

But Noah didn't flinch. God had told him to build the ship because He was going to destroy the earth due to humanity's wickedness. Therefore Noah set about his ark-building task with precision and determination. A boat that size would have taken a long time to be built by one man and his three sons. There are guesstimates that it took fifty-five to seventy-five years to build. That's a long time. But God was transforming Noah's loneliness into persistence. And that persistence brought about the preservation of human and animal life—including his own life and the lives of his family.

Might God transform your loneliness into persistence in your obedience to Him? Partner with God in your loneliness and invite Him to transform you.

The Man Whose Loneliness Was Transformed into Trust

Daniel was alone when he defied the mighty King Darius of Persia. The king had been manipulated by Daniel's enemies into making a decree that no one could petition (pray to) anyone other than the king for thirty days. Daniel's enemies figured they had Daniel trapped because they knew him to be faithful to his God alone. The consequences for disobeying this decree? Being thrown into a den of hungry lions. The king signed the decree into law and sealed it with his signet ring—and anything sealed with that ring could not be revoked.

Daniel was aware of the new law, and yet what did he do? Without hesitation, he continued his habit of praying in his room three times a day. Not behind closed doors or under cover. No. With the windows wide open toward Jerusalem. Anyone who wanted to "catch" Daniel didn't have to come upon him stealthily. He was praying to his God in plain sight.

Daniel was alone in his faithfulness to God. All alone.

It didn't take long for the conniving bunch to go straight to the king to tell him what Daniel was doing in defiance of the king's irrevocable law. Daniel would have to be thrown into the lions' den. This was not something the great King Darius wanted to do, but he was caught by his own law. It could not be changed. The king said to Daniel, "Your God whom you constantly serve will Himself deliver you" (Dan. 6:16). What a statement of faith from the king of Persia! Daniel had clearly already had a powerful influence on the pagan king even though he was one man and took a lonely stand.

As per the law, Daniel was thrown into the lions' den. He was alone facing those fierce, hungry lions. Was he afraid? Of course! We all would be. Any minute a hungry beast might tear him to shreds. In the Sunday school pictures of my childhood, I remember Daniel standing tall and erect, and he seems so calm. But in reality, it must have been a fearsome scene. He didn't just calmly walk into a nice cave. He was roughly thrown into a pit. I imagine the men who devised this scheme would have been only too happy to rough Daniel up on the way there. And the lions were hungry, gnashing their teeth and roaring. Have you ever heard a lion's roar? It's deep and echoes like thunder. These roars would have reverberated around that den. Deafening. The lions wanted some meat. They wanted dinner.

And here comes Daniel—fresh meat! But just then an angel shows up! How dramatic is that? Daniel calls him God's angel. That is a powerful, mighty creature who serves as a ministering servant of the Most High God. No doubt he got the lions' attention, and they shut up. The roaring ceased. They quieted. Then what do you think happened? Did the angel just leave? I don't think so. I think he stayed. Using my imagination, I wonder if he discussed with Daniel what was happening in the world. Maybe they talked of God's plans. Maybe they played with the lions, compared the size of their jaws, felt their manes, pet them. The angel refreshed Daniel. He encouraged him. Certainly, he would have let Daniel know God had been listening to Daniel's prayers and was pleased with his faithfulness. Angels have done this from time to time as messengers of God. When Jesus was tempted in the wilderness for forty days and nights, we are told that "angels came and began to minister to Him" (Matt. 4:11). And again when Jesus was in the Garden of Gethsemane, we are told, "Now an angel from heaven appeared to Him, strengthening Him" (Luke 22:43).

Meanwhile, King Darius had a miserable night. He "spent the night fasting, and no entertainment was brought before him; and his sleep fled from him" (Dan. 6:18). As soon as it was dawn, he ran to the lions' den to check on Daniel. Perhaps he expected bloody remains and bones strewn about. He called out with an anxious voice, "Daniel, servant of the living God, has your God, whom you constantly serve, been able to deliver you from the lions?" (v. 20). I love that! God was the One who created the lions in the first place—of course He was able to deliver Daniel. Out of the darkness, from the lions' den, came a strong, clear voice. "O king, live forever! My God sent His angel and shut the lions' mouths and they have not harmed me" (vv. 21–22).

"So Daniel was taken up out of the den and no injury whatever was found on him, because he had trusted in his God" (v. 23). The loneliness that Daniel endured out of his faithfulness to God was transformed into trust.

Might God transform your loneliness into trust in Him? Partner with God in your loneliness and invite that transformation.

The Man Whose Loneliness Was Transformed into Intimacy with God

We often hear the phrase "the patience of Job." Who was Job? Why did he need patience? We learn about Job in the Old Testament, and James also talks about him in his epistle in the New Testament. Job was a very rich man considered righteous by God Himself. And yet God allowed untold suffering into his life. Job lost nearly everything. Literally. All his many servants. All his livestock and thus his livelihood. Worse, his ten children were all killed at once. Soon after, he lost his health. And while he did not lose his wife, the stress and calamities drove a wedge between them.

Three of his friends came to visit him in his misery. For a whole week, they said nothing. "They sat down on the ground with him for seven days and seven nights with no one speaking a word to him, for they saw that his pain was very great" (Job 2:13). That was the best thing they could do—just be present with him. But after seven days had passed, they couldn't help themselves. They began to try to explain to Job the reasons for his suffering. They insisted the innocent do not suffer, that God is just and rewards those who are good. They concluded, then, that Job must have sinned greatly to have such disasters fall on him. They continued to add to his misery by preaching at him about God's ways. They rebuked him. They accused him of unrighteousness.

How lonely Job must have been in his anguish! His "friends" didn't understand Job's situation nor his heart of faithfulness to God. They thought they understood God's ways but had completely missed the truth.

Job maintained his innocence as he sat in the ash heap, covered in boils, scraping them with bits of pottery. He had lots of questions and no answers. He didn't understand why so many evils had befallen him. The answers he'd thought he had didn't hold up in the face of so much tragedy. The only thing he felt he knew for certain was that he had done the very best he could to trust God and live righteously.

In spite of being in the presence of friends, Job was bereft. And alone. Yet, still, he held on to his faith in God. Perhaps only by his fingernails.

Finally, he couldn't take his friends' endless pontificating any longer and let it all out. He let it rip. He said to them, "I will not restrain my mouth; I will speak in the anguish of my spirit, I will complain in the bitterness of my soul" (7:11). He cursed the day he was born. He believed his life was futile. He despaired of God and his "friends."

But after a long exchange, he declares to them: "As for me, I know that my Redeemer lives, and at the last He will take His stand on the earth" (19:25). Wow. What a statement after all he'd been through. Job had a solid assurance of where he ultimately stood. But that assurance didn't keep him from feeling the pain or the loneliness of all he'd lost.

Finally, Job declared that he wanted to meet with God—face-to-face. "Oh that I knew where I might find Him, that I might come to His seat! I would present my case before Him and fill my mouth with arguments" (23:3–4). He built a case against God's way of dealing with things. He was confused and wanted to express His confusion directly to God.

In our aloneness, we need to express our feelings to God Himself. Just let it all out. If need be, set a chair opposite of you and imagine the Lord sitting in it. Have a conversation with Him. Tell Him how you are feeling—the good, the bad, and the ugly. Angry confrontation doesn't upset Him. He loves us as a good Father. He wants us to fully and completely share our hearts with Him, not holding back. After all, He knows all about us, knows what we are thinking and feeling anyway. We cannot hide our true feelings from Him. Trevor Hudson writes,

> Polite prayer poisons our relationship with God. Honest prayer involves stating our doubts and disappointments, our anger and resentment, our loneliness and grief . . . the purpose of being transparent with God is not to give information to God. The purpose is to develop intimacy with God.[7]

Have you ever before considered that expressing your loneliness to God may be a pathway to greater intimacy with Him?

But in the meantime, we may still experience times of loneliness. *Let's remember loneliness isn't an eternal condition. It is temporary. It will end.* And for those of us who have placed our trust in the Lord Jesus, we know the future is glorious. When we are alone, it is good to have that assurance. We know our Redeemer lives. We know what the future holds. As my mother used to say, "I've read the last chapter and I know who wins!"

As Paul puts it, "For momentary, light affliction is producing for us an eternal weight of glory far beyond all comparison" (2 Cor. 4:17). Paul goes on to say in verse 18, "We look not at the things which are seen, but at the things which are not seen; for the things which are seen are temporal, but the things which are not seen are eternal." It's vital to keep eternity in view when we are lonely.

Speaking of "things unseen," in Job chapters 38–41 the Lord finally answers Job. Does He provide the reason for Job's suffering? No, He does not. Instead He refocuses Job's attention on the unseen—on the magnificence, the power, the mysteries, and the goodness of the eternal God—to the point where Job cries out, "I have declared that which I did not understand, things too wonderful for me, which I did not know" (Job 42:3). Job then retracts his accusations against God and declares "now my eye sees You" (v. 5).

And that is one insight we need in order to endure our own loneliness. Though we may not see the *why* of our temporary loneliness, may we keep our eyes on *Who* transforms our loneliness. May we do as Job did and honestly communicate our hearts to God, not to *inform* Him but to increase our intimacy with Him so we see Him more clearly.

God transformed Job's loneliness into a new intimacy with Him.

Will you allow God to transform your loneliness into new intimacy with Him too? Partner with God in your loneliness and invite that transformation.

Choosing Partnership in the Transformation of Your Loneliness

I hope you notice in this chapter that I'm not suggesting you simply conjure up Noah's persistence, Daniel's trust, or Job's intimacy with God. It was *God* who did the transforming, not them! But in each case that transformation took place as a result of a choice that His beloved follower made. Noah partnered with God by choosing obedience. Daniel partnered with God by choosing faithfulness. Job partnered with God by choosing honest and open communication. And it was God who caused each transformation.

Young Jane Merchant, my dear mother, and my adolescent self made choices to partner with God as well. That is the choice before you now. You can do the same. You can choose to receive loneliness as a red flag that something's got to change, as a gift that will surprise you, as a pathway to holiness that will draw you closer to God and even, as we will explore, draw you closer to others. Before you turn the page to the next chapter, I pray that you will invite God to transform your loneliness into His eternal purposes.

And we all, who with unveiled faces
contemplate the Lord's glory, are being
transformed into his image with ever-
increasing glory, which comes from the Lord,
who is the Spirit.

2 Corinthians 3:18 NIV

The Treasures of Solitude

Language has created the word loneliness to express the pain of being alone, and the word solitude to express the glory of being alone.

Paul Tillich[1]

I had three very excited small children. They had arisen before dawn that morning—it was Christmas Day! We lived on what I would have called a fifty-acre farm, but in Texas it was called a ranch.

My husband had made plans to go hunting in South Texas that afternoon and the days that followed. I had asked him not to. I was so tired. With all the preparation for Christmas— decorating, shopping, wrapping, cleaning, cooking—I was all used up. I wanted him to at least stay and enjoy the rest of the day with the family. He could go the next day, I'd urged. But he refused. He packed his hunting gear and loaded it up in the back of his pickup truck, and off he went. I watched him drive away, too tired to be angry. The kids, playing with their new toys, were oblivious to my sadness.

I picked up the house and cleaned the kitchen—putting things back in order. I had a sad heart. Why would he leave me alone on Christmas, of all days? He was often gone, traveling for work. But did he have to travel on Christmas? I knew he didn't. It was his choice. I wondered how I would spend the quiet, lonely night after the kids were in bed. In my book, Christmas was the time to be with family. And here I was, miles away from my family, and my husband was out hunting. I tried not to slip into feeling sorry for myself in my loneliness, but I felt the familiar tug of those emotions drawing me downward.

Do you know the feeling—that descent into a dark place you really want to avoid and hate the feeling that it's not in your power to stop it? We've talked a lot in recent chapters about God seeing us in our loneliness and His power to intervene in our lives; about all we have in common with others in the world who, like us, struggle with loneliness; about partnering with God to transform our loneliness into His purposes. But this is where the rubber hits the road, isn't it? Circumstances beyond our control crash into our lives, upending our hopes and expectations for connection and a sense of closeness. And there we are. Alone *and* lonely.

What happens if God doesn't transform our loneliness into something else? (Or at least not on our preferred time-table.) What if we do our best to partner with Him and He doesn't change anything at all? (At least not that we can see.) Then what? Are we simply stuck? What do we do with our dark emotions and thoughts? Are we to just grit our teeth and bear being lonely?

I confess that I slipped into a foul mood. Hoping that my husband would be sensitive to my needs had gotten me nowhere. I wanted to reach out to someone, but the last thing I desired was to pick up the phone on Christmas Day and call someone and complain. It was hard to imagine that God would transform my loneliness into something positive and useful, but He'd done it before in my boarding school days. Though this event happened many years ago, I remember it well, and looking back I marvel at what God did for me that Christmas night.

I had made a list of the many lovely gifts I'd received that season and decided I would begin to write my thank-you notes. So many family members and friends had been generous and creative. I liked to write thank-you notes, and thought it would be a pleasant way to spend the evening. As I wrote one note of gratitude after another, my heart grew lighter. I was grateful for the love expressed to us by so many. And I had three precious children all snug in their own beds, finally asleep! The house was quiet. Note after note. Until all were finished. That meant the need to find time to write notes wouldn't be hanging over my head for weeks and everyone would get a prompt "thank you." This was great!

The evening was still relatively young, and my heart was now much lighter thanks to practicing gratitude, so I decided to sit down and play the piano. We had a baby grand in the living room, and though I'd had lessons as a young girl, I did not actually play well. I could, however, pick out the notes. I pulled out the hymnbook and looked at the list of Christmas carols—so many favorites, but perhaps my very favorite was "Thou Didst Leave Thy Throne" by Emily S. Elliott. It isn't sung very much in churches today, but it remains a favorite of mine.

Thou didst leave Thy throne and Thy kingly crown,
When Thou camest to earth for me;
But in Bethlehem's home was there found no room
For Thy holy nativity.
O come to my heart, Lord Jesus,
There is room in my heart for Thee.[2]

I sat in my living room, plunking out that tune, worshiping the One who had come to earth for me. Though I was all alone, I knew I wasn't really. God inhabits the praises of His people, and He did that night. I had so dreaded that Christmas evening by myself, but I now recall it as one of my happiest Christmas memories. Somehow, in a way that only God could, He'd tenderly lifted the loneliness out of me as I'd stopped fighting it and turned my energies to giving thanks. There was room in my heart for Him! Without even knowing what to call it, I'd honored God by worshiping Him in song and praise.

And I'd done so not in loneliness, but in *solitude*.

The Rich Rewards of Solitude

People often equate loneliness and solitude, but in truth they are quite different. I agree with author Hara Estroff Marano, who wrote in *Psychology Today*,

> There is a world of difference between solitude and loneliness, though the two terms are often used interchangeably. From the outside, solitude and loneliness look a lot alike. Both are characterized by solitariness. But all resemblance ends at the surface.... Loneliness is a negative state, marked by a sense of isolation.... Solitude is the state of being

alone without being lonely. . . . Solitude is a time that can be
used for reflection, inner searching or growth or enjoyment
of some kind.³

Another way to put it is that loneliness tends to feel like an
excess of alone time and is marked by feeling discontented.
Solitude, on the other hand, tends to feel peaceful. It seems
to surface from a rich inner life. It replenishes us, renews us,
and refreshes us. When we choose to spend time in solitude,
we can use that time to explore our hearts and minds and
get to know ourselves and our God better—to come away
with a fresh perspective. Marano also said, "Solitude restores
body and mind. Loneliness depletes them."⁴ I would add that
solitude restores our spirits as well.

The question I suggest we explore, then, is this: If loneliness is so negative and solitude so positive, can we actually
change our loneliness into solitude?

What do you think? Both are the state of being alone. It
begins there. I tend to think of solitude as something we
choose, whereas loneliness is a feeling that comes over us
unbidden. But once loneliness has arrived on our doorstep,
can we transform it into solitude? Elisabeth Elliot seemed
to think so. She wrote, "Turn your loneliness into solitude,
and your solitude into prayer."⁵ Isn't that what happened to
me that Christmas night in Texas? I moved from lonely to
grateful to singing God's praises. But did that come about
by a choice I made, or did God transform my loneliness into
solitude? Perhaps it was an interplay of both?

I like to think of solitude as making room in our souls
for God by shutting down all the noise of the demands on
our lives and opening ourselves up to His influence on our

thoughts, feelings, and ideas that have been living below the surface for too long.

Of course, not everyone needs the same balance of solitude and connection with others. One article said,

> By actively taking the time to be in isolation [note that I would say "solitude" rather than "isolation"] it allows us to find balance. Extroverted people live primarily on social life, whereas introverted people tolerate loneliness much better. Both ultimately need a certain amount of solitude to find harmony.[6]

Solitude, therefore, is not a one-size-fits-all exercise. We have to experiment to explore the healthy balance that suits us, and we may very well find that balance shifts with various seasons of our lives.

I came across a rather sad piece of information as I was researching solitude. The Google Ngram Viewer or Google Books Ngram Viewer is an online search engine that charts the frequencies of use of any set of words or phrases. How telling it is that Google Ngram reveals a decrease in the use of the word *solitude* while at the same time use of the word *loneliness* has increased.[7] The reality is that if we devote ourselves intentionally to solitude with God, we can actually decrease our loneliness. We'll explore how, in this and the next chapter.

I wasn't surprised to find that science positioned solitude as being focused solely on self, while I, focusing on the spiritual experience of solitude, saw it as a time for spiritual intimacy with God. Keeping that difference in mind, however, let's look at five "science-based benefits of solitude" according to author Anne-Laure Le Cunff:

1. Increased productivity
2. More meaningful relationships
3. Better mental strength
4. More creativity
5. Self-transformation

"In the end," writes Le Cunff, "it all boils down to being intentional in the way we approach solitude. . . . Solitude can be a mindful activity, if you decided to dedicate time to it."[8]

If science can identify those benefits, how many more benefits might we identify as believers in an eternal soul? Well, let's take a look at some biblical examples of solitude and see what we discover.

David, a Man Who Nurtured Solitude

The story of David and Goliath is perhaps one of the most famous Bible stories. It is even referred to in secular settings such as business. But can you imagine what it was like for David to defy this massive man—almost ten feet tall—suited up in bronze armor? He must have looked like a monster as his armor glistened in the sun and his voice boomed across the valley between the two war-ready armies. He was defying the living God of Israel. And not one of Saul's soldiers would stand up to him.

David was young. He was a shepherd. He had not been trained for war. But he was no weakling—he had killed a lion and a bear with his bare hands. He had spent hours alone tending sheep and engaging in target practice. Writing songs. Talking to God. Listening to God.

David loved God and could not stand to hear Him mocked by this godless Philistine, so he volunteered to go against Goliath—taking only his stick and five smooth stones, which he put in his bag along with his slingshot. His brothers thought it was a joke and so did the giant. We see David's brothers' reaction to him when he visited them in the army:

> Now Eliab his oldest brother heard when he spoke to the men; and Eliab's anger burned against David and he said, "Why have you come down? And with whom have you left those few sheep in the wilderness? I know your insolence and the wickedness of your heart; for you have come down in order to see the battle." (1 Sam. 17:28)

His own brothers had no respect or concern for him. He was "just a shepherd."

The giant mocked him, "'Am I a dog, that you come to me with sticks?' And the Philistine cursed David by his gods" (v. 43). The armies on both sides heard and watched. David was by himself—a small, lone figure. But he was confident God was with him. He knew the victory was his. He refused to let this giant intimidate him or hurl insults at God. We are told that "David ran quickly toward the battle line to meet the Philistine" (v. 48). And the rest is history.

All the hours young David had spent in solitude had not been wasted. Nor need ours be.

We read a lot about young David of Israel. He spent a lot of time alone out in the fields as a shepherd protecting his sheep. Being a shepherd was not a coveted position. As a matter of fact, people looked down on shepherds as lowlifes.

When the prophet Samuel had gone to Bethlehem to anoint a new king over Israel (before the Goliath incident) he went to the home of Jesse (David's father). God had given clear instruction as to what Samuel was to do. God was going to show him the new king of Israel, and he was to anoint him there and then. Jesse paraded his sons one by one in front of Samuel. The prophet was impressed with each one, but God didn't choose any of them. He told Samuel, "God sees not as man sees, for man looks at the outward appearance, but the LORD looks at the heart" (16:7).

Finally, after all seven had come before Samuel, he told Jesse that God had not chosen any of them. Then he asked Jesse if that was all his sons. Jesse said, "There remains yet the youngest, and behold, he is tending the sheep" (v. 11). What if Samuel had not inquired? He did inquire because God had told him he was to go to Bethlehem, to Jesse's house, to anoint a king from among his sons. David's family may have let it slide; after all, he was the youngest. He was tending sheep. He wasn't important. But when David was brought in from the fields, "Samuel took the horn of oil and anointed him in the midst of his brothers, and the Spirit of the LORD came mightily upon David from that day forward" (v. 13).

Someone knew David was a skilled harpist and recommended he play for King Saul, so he began to serve the king in that way. His playing soothed the troubled soul of the king. You don't become the king's harpist unless you are extremely talented. Where did he learn that skill? He must have practiced his playing out in the fields while tending the sheep, perhaps at night under the stars. Bringing down the giant showed he was also skilled with the sling. He must have practiced by the hour to become so accurate. I think it's fair to say David spent a lot of time alone, and he used that time to grow his skills.

He was only a young man when he slayed Goliath with his slingshot, which thrust him into international fame. He went on to become a great warrior and military tactician. He was a remarkable man. The women would sing, "Saul has slain his thousands, and David his ten thousands" (18:7). That did not play well in the palace. King Saul became jealous of David. We know he had to flee from King Saul's presence because Saul was so angry and jealous.

David wrote many psalms, or songs, in his solitude—some of them the most beautiful written language in the world, rich with imagery. We know from these psalms he knew the utter loneliness of God's absence. God wasn't absent, but it felt that way to David: "How long, O LORD? Will You forget me forever? How long will You hide Your face from me? How long shall I take counsel in my soul, having sorrow in my heart all the day?" (Ps. 13:1–2). But David also loved to praise God. "My heart shall rejoice in Your salvation. I will sing to the LORD, because He has dealt bountifully with me" (vv. 5–6).

The principal theme of the book of Psalms is worship.

The songs reflect many of the circumstances we face in life: difficulty and danger, sickness and the fear of death, failure and sin and defeat. But they also sing of joy, deliverance, victory and triumph, always with an awareness of God's attributes of love, goodness and power.[9]

Still today many of the psalms are sung. Many are memorized. Who of us doesn't know of Psalm 23?

Like David, we have a choice when we are alone: to wallow in our loneliness or to be productive. Solitude can be the breeding ground for great thinking, writing, learning. But we need to find a balance. We don't want to simply "get busy" to fill the lonely hours or we may miss God's voice. "Lonely times are preparatory times, but we will be able to see this and embrace the goodness of it if we make God's purposes our own," writes Lydia Brownback.[10]

David was a busy man. No doubt about that. He became a warrior king with enemies on every side. But he valued above all else the time he spent with God. He wrote, "As the deer pants for the water brooks, so my soul pants for You, O God" (Ps. 42:1), and "Whom have I in heaven but You? And besides You, I desire nothing on earth" (73:25). He used his solitude to develop a close relationship with God, just like we can. He invested his solitude in honing his skills. His solitude was productive. Ours can be too.

As I reflect on these many ways that David so productively used his solitude—from exploring and honing his physical skills, to fostering his creativity through composing poetry and music, to nourishing his relationship with God—I'd describe him as a man who nurtured his solitude. So I'm inspired to choose to nurture my soul as well.

Can we transform our feelings of sad loneliness into times of productive solitude that we, too, can nurture? I believe we can. We begin by giving our loneliness to God in prayer. Just tell Him you're lonely and you want to work with Him in transforming your loneliness into productive solitude. Ask for His help. And then nourish your solitude with praise by simply beginning to praise Him. Turn to the Psalms for ways to praise Him. Look at Psalm 147 and 148 to guide you. You may also want to use the prayers and verses in appendix C. Beginning today, you, like David, can choose to nurture productive solitude.

John on Patmos, a Man Devoted to Drawing Close to God

Richard Foster wrote, "The purpose of solitude is to be able to see and hear."[11] That's what I want to do! I want to see and hear God more clearly than I ever have before.

"But you, when you pray, go into your inner room, close your door, and pray to your Father who is in secret, and your Father who sees what is done in secret will reward you" (Matt. 6:6). These were Jesus's words just before He taught His disciples how to pray using what we call the Lord's Prayer. The purpose of going into our inner room—or we can call it our prayer closet—is to close the door on all outward distractions. To be able to pray to the Father "who is in secret." I've heard people say they can't find God. Maybe they are not looking where He is! God is already waiting for you in that secret place and will meet you there. It is important to get alone with God—to draw near to Him.

Perhaps no disciple better demonstrates the value of drawing near to God than John. John wrote, "God is love" (1 John 4:8). In fact, he was one of the three people closest to Jesus. We know that on the last night Jesus was with His disciples, the night of the Last Supper, John was sitting right next to Jesus, "reclining on Jesus's bosom" (John 13:23). We also know that even before he met Jesus John was devoting himself to seeing and hearing as much about God as he could, because he first followed John the Baptist. But when he heard

John the Baptist say, "Behold, the Lamb of God!" (1:36) he and Andrew, Peter's brother, immediately began to follow Jesus. When Jesus saw them following Him, He asked what they wanted. They said they wanted to know where Jesus was staying; He told them to come and see. They did. And it changed their lives.

John's last years were spent in Ephesus. He wrote five books of the New Testament, making him second only to the apostle Paul as the most prolific New Testament writer. As a result of anti-Christian persecution under the Roman emperor Domitian, John was exiled to the island of Patmos for his missionary activities. He was there "because of the word of God and the testimony of Jesus" (Rev. 1:9).

Patmos is a small island off of what is now Turkey, not far from Ephesus. John was aging with all the discomforts that come with that. To be exiled means to be expelled from one's native land or home by an authoritative decree. My dictionary uses such words as *banished*, *expulsion*, and *separated*. Not inviting words. John was away from all that was familiar and beloved. Away from loved ones. Alone. But while he was alone, John writes that he "was in the Spirit on the Lord's day" (v. 10). I love that! No pity party for him. He was worshiping. He was seeking God.

John had a choice. He could have chosen to be angry and resentful. After all, as a faithful, close follower, he'd been with Jesus. He was there at the foot of the cross. He was commissioned by Jesus Himself to care for His mother. And because of his faithfulness to sharing the Good News about Jesus he was stuck on this island surrounded by the sea, banished to this seemingly godforsaken island. Yet he chose to devote this time of solitude to allow God to do something in and through him for His purposes. And what purposes they were!

The young church was undergoing persecution. God wanted His people to know He was in their midst and involved in the affairs of mankind. He wanted to get that message to them. Who could He trust? Who could He use? John! John, the beloved disciple. God began to reveal things to John through an angel, much like He had done with Ezekiel and Daniel. These revelations were mind-blowing, to say the least. They were apocalyptic and are difficult to understand. What we learn from them is that God has a plan. He is in control of what is happening and what will happen.

John knew that firsthand as a disciple. He had seen and heard so many things as he followed Jesus: the demoniac cleansed, Lazarus raised from the dead, Peter walking on the water, five thousand–plus people fed from just five loaves and two fish. He didn't understand any of it—but he trusted and loved Jesus.

The revelations he received on Patmos were things he did not really comprehend. They were "otherworldly." But John wrote them down as God had commanded him to: "Write in a book what you see, and send it to the seven churches" (v. 11).

John was isolated and alone. Surrounded by the ocean as far as the eye could see. As much as I love the ocean, John didn't. One of the distinctive features of the new heaven and new earth, John tells us, is "there is no longer any sea" (21:1). He'd had his fill! Though banished for doing what Jesus told him to do, that didn't stop him. He continued to worship God, even all by himself. And he was obedient to God's call on his life. That call wasn't what he expected. It wasn't what he'd planned. But he allowed God to use his life as He wanted. He abandoned his life and desires to God.

We are told that the revelation he had was on the Lord's Day. John was keeping the routine of observing the Lord's Day and worshiping. We can do the same—even if we are alone. In our times of loneliness, do we still worship? Do we draw close to God that we might see and hear Him more clearly? What better time to draw closer to God than those moments we are alone and lonely? There is no interference when we are alone. It is such an opportunity to worship without any self-consciousness because there is no one to hear you sing, shout, pray out loud, or cry. The decision to use your lonely moments to draw closer to God can transform your loneliness into rich solitude. He promises He will more than fill up your empty spaces and give you a clearer vision of who He is. Beginning today, you can choose to draw close to God in your solitude that you may see and hear Him as never before.

Solitude is intentional. Loneliness is not. Solitude is invited. Loneliness is dreaded. Solitude has a purpose. Loneliness is endured. Like David and John, choose to devote your lonely times to God's purposes, and they will be transformed from the emptiness of loneliness to the treasures of solitude.

Draw near to God and He will draw near to you.

James 4:8 NKJV

8

The Cultivation of Solitude

Solitude is a place where Christ remodels us in his own image and frees us from the victimizing compulsions of the world.

Henri Nouwen[1]

I made my way down the long hospital corridor, not knowing what I was going to see when I finally entered my husband's room in the ICU. During the long two-hour drive from home, I'd nervously tried to prepare myself for the worst. All the nurse had told me by phone was that my husband had been in a serious car crash and I was needed as soon as possible. Now that I was actually here, I was surprised at the calm that settled over me like a blanket. I was alone, but I didn't feel alone at all. God's presence was palpable. I have no other words to describe it other than an overwhelming sense of God's presence. I *knew* I was in the palm of His hand. In all my years before and since, I'd never felt anything quite like it.

The moment I stepped into his room I understood why God was ministering to me so tangibly. If they had not told me the man in the bed was my husband, I would not have recognized him. His face was swollen to the size of a large pumpkin. He was comatose and hooked up to several monitors and oxygen. He had a neck collar on, and all sorts of machines were beeping and whirling. Tubes ran from everywhere. Even as I met with the doctors, God's presence didn't leave me. It was hard for me to absorb the news that my husband's very survival was on the line, and that if he did survive, his injuries would require significant care for months to come—or longer. They explained that his left arm might need to be amputated and that he currently had no kidney function. He'd clearly be in the hospital for some time. The doctors would do all they could. My role was to stay by his bedside and pray.

Since I lived so far away, the hospital arranged for me to stay at a nearby hospitality house. I quickly settled into a routine. Every morning I arrived, alone, at the hospital early enough to catch the morning rounds of the doctors, and there I stayed, alone, until evening when I'd walk back to the hospitality house. My days were spent by the side of my mostly unconscious or sleeping husband. I quickly got to know the many nurses, medical aids, and doctors who formed a steady, never-ending parade through the room.

Had the accident happened near home, close to my local hospital, I'm sure I would have been kept company by a stream of visitors—family and friends and church members—but my three adult children lived many hours away, and my husband's three children, substantially younger, lived with their mother hours away as well. Many people did make the drive the night of the accident to pray with me, and occasionally people would stop by as they were able. I was grateful to those who came. As days turned into weeks all the children were able to visit, but for the most part I stood vigil alone.

It was a long and lonely ordeal, but now as I've worked on this book, I can see that God really did help me transform much of that loneliness into solitude. I immersed myself in prayer, and not only did I read and study my Bible but I read several other books and did a fair amount of writing too. In addition, I kept a journal in which I recorded the spiritual insights and growth I was experiencing. I also played Christian music in the room—not only for my husband's benefit but to keep me focused on praise. And I connected to so many people through email and phone that I was able to nurture a number of relationships as they ministered to me. Praise God for the marvelous network of prayer warriors all over the country who held us up in prayer.

Ever so slowly my husband's condition improved. Rather than being spiritually depleted by the entire ordeal, by the time he was released from the hospital I felt that I came away from it spiritually richer. I felt an intimate connection with the Lord.

Intimacy and connection, with God and with others— isn't that what we were made for? And those are the very opposite of loneliness.

Here are a few practical suggestions for stepping into a time of solitude. First, I suggest starting with words of praise. I've found memorizing verses from the Psalms to be a very helpful tool. You might want to start with these:

> "O satisfy us in the morning with Your lovingkindness, that we may sing for joy and be glad all our days." (90:14)

"O LORD, our Lord, how majestic is Your name in all the earth, who have displayed Your splendor above the heavens!" (8:1)

"I will give thanks to the LORD with all my heart; I will tell of all Your wonders. I will be glad and exult in You; I will sing praise to Your name, O Most High." (9:1–2)

"'I love You, O LORD, my strength.' The LORD is my rock and my fortress and my deliverer, my God, my rock, in whom I take refuge; my shield and the horn of my salvation, my stronghold. I call upon the LORD, who is worthy to be praised." (18:1–3)

When you offer words of praise to God it changes your focus from you to Him. It spurs you on to appreciate that He is with you and you belong to Him. That He is your Daddy and your Lord. Here's an idea for your next time of solitude with the Lord: go through the book of Psalms and select several verses of praise that really speak to you about belonging to the Lord. Memorize them. Pray them back to God. Print them out and put them on your mirror and daily go over them until they are yours.

Second, spend time with God. That means time in prayer, time in the Word, and time in solitude. Here's some great advice from the writer of Hebrews: "Through Him then, let us continually offer up a sacrifice of praise to God, that is, the fruit of lips that give thanks to His name" (Heb. 13:15). Yes. *Continually* is the key word here. When you are lonely, you need to remind yourself that God is your Daddy and daily companion. I often play Christian music because it inspires me to praise God and sets the tone of my home even if I am alone.

Finally, I try to memorize Scripture so that it is readily available to me. It also keeps my mind active and focused on God's Word. As I get older, memorizing is not as easy as it used to be, unfortunately. But my mother was such an example to me of Scripture memorizing. She would memorize whole chapters of Scripture at a time, and did so up until her last days. She was memorizing Psalm 90 close to her death at the age of eighty-seven. How appropriate: "Lord, You have been our dwelling place in all generations. Before the mountains were born or You gave birth to the earth and the world, even from everlasting to everlasting, You are God" (vv. 1–2). She would often quote that passage and talk about the faithfulness of God.

In the previous chapter we observed how David *nurtured* productive solitude in his life and how John *devoted* his solitude to drawing close to God that he might see and hear the voice of God. Now let's turn our eyes to the ultimate expert on *cultivating* solitude. Who better to teach us how to nourish our intimacy with God than Jesus?

Slipping Away

Jesus loved people. He partied with them, wept with them, fished with them, told them stories, fed them, touched them, and healed them. "But Jesus Himself would *often* slip away to the wilderness and pray" (Luke 5:16, emphasis added). And not just to the wilderness! The Gospels record that Jesus made a habit of slipping away to the wilderness, the mountains, the sea, and the garden. And He did so to take a break not just from the crowds but from His disciples as well. Clearly it was a priority for Jesus to spend time in solitude.

Matthew, Mark, Luke, and John all emphasize Jesus's choice to devote time to solitude, and they often give us the context of what was happening in the life and ministry of Jesus at the time. Matthew tells us of the time when Jesus had just heard the news of the violent death of his cousin, John the Baptist. No doubt He was greatly saddened. "Now when Jesus heard about John, He withdrew from there in a boat to a secluded place by Himself" (Matt. 14:13). He was grieving. However, the crowds followed Jesus, and He had compassion on them. They were tired and hungry. He took all day to minister to their needs, and by evening they needed to be fed. So He did that too. He fed five thousand people with five loaves of bread and two fish. They crowded Him, jostled Him, hung on Him, and stepped on His toes. He was constantly meeting the needs of others. Constantly giving of Himself.

But then He refreshed Himself with solitude. He got alone with God. He talked to God about all that was on His heart and mind. "After He had sent the crowds away, He went up on the mountain by Himself to pray; and when it was evening, He was there alone" (v. 23).

Sometimes we have to send the "crowds" away too. Though we might be lonely, our thoughts and worries and needs crowd our minds. Our busy schedules occupy our attention. We, too, need to choose solitude with God and talk to Him. Not some fancy prayer, with big words all theologically correct and formally composed and uttered. How stilted that would be! He wants us to just be ourselves and speak to Him like we would to a friend—because He *is* our friend: "I have called you friends, for all things that I have heard from My Father I have made known to you" (John 15:15).

And the amazing thing? God speaks back because He is our friend. We saw in an earlier chapter that Abraham was called a friend of God. And look at this verse about Moses: "Thus the LORD used to speak to Moses face to face, just as a man speaks to his friend" (Exod. 33:11). When we are talking with a friend it is not a one-sided monologue. No. We talk and we listen.

For Jesus, His time with God was leisurely. He didn't rush through it. He spent all night with God—talking and listening. It was a necessity for Jesus to talk with His Father. And if it was a necessity for Him who is one with God, how much more necessary is it for us?

When we are praying, talking to our Friend, we are not lonely. We are in His company. Use your imagination. Picture Him in the room with you—because He is. He is smiling at you. His eyes are full of love and compassion. There is no judgment there. Take a deep breath. Let out your thoughts, feelings, and needs and sense His overwhelming peace. Talk with Him about things that grate on you and bug you. About the big things. Decisions you have to make. Questions you have. Talk openly and freely. Talk out loud, if that's easier. Don't measure your words. But I would caution you—He is a holy God and to be respected. Don't treat Him casually or presumptuously. King David prayed that God would keep Him from presumptuous sins.

> Also keep back Your servant from presumptuous
>   sins;
> Let them not rule over me;
> Then I will be blameless,
> And I shall be acquitted of great transgression.

> Let the words of my mouth and the meditation of
>   my heart
> Be acceptable in Your sight,
> O Lord, my rock and my Redeemer. (Ps. 19:13–14)

We don't have to wonder how Jesus talked to His Father. In John 17 we have what is often called His "High Priestly Prayer." In it Jesus asked that God be glorified in all He had done and taught. And He asked His Father to glorify Him, Jesus, because He had accomplished God's purpose on earth. He prayed for His disciples that God would keep them. Then He prayed for those in the future who would believe because of the disciples' testimony—that's you and me. He prayed for the unity of all who believe and asked that God's love would be in us.

I've barely scratched the surface of what we know of Jesus cultivating solitude. To *cultivate* means to prepare, tend, manage, fertilize, and enrich. He did all that and more in His time alone. As I see it, He *inhabited* that solitude, meaning to abide in, dwell in, occupy, lodge, or nest. Those are rich words to stretch your understanding of what solitude with God is all about.

I invite you to look up some other verses about Jesus and the time He devoted to solitude with His Father. I love Mark 1:35: "In the early morning, while it was still dark, Jesus got up, left the house, and went away to a secluded place, and was praying there." In Mark 3:7 He "withdrew" to the sea—one of my favorite places. In Mark 6:30–32, after He had sent the twelve disciples to do ministry, upon their return He invited them to "come away" with Him to rest and recharge. And in Mark 6:45–47 Jesus went up on a mountain by Himself, and when evening came He was still there.

We see a glorious moment of Jesus in communion with His Father when, in Mark 9:2, He invites Peter, James, and John to come away with Him "by themselves" to witness the transfiguration, where Jesus became brilliantly radiant in all His glory and Elijah and Moses appeared with Him. And in Luke we see Jesus prepare in solitude before choosing the twelve (Luke 6:12–13). Yes, Jesus used solitude with His Father to refresh and recharge, to heal from grief, to prepare for major decisions, to bask in the glory of His Father—and we can do the same. The writers of the Gospels recorded it all. But of all the instances in Scripture of Jesus cultivating solitude with God, I believe that John, His beloved friend, best captured the most poignant, intimate, and powerful time of Jesus's solitude of all—in the Garden of Gethsemane.

Gethsemane

I write this with a sense of reverence because Gethsemane is holy ground. Like Moses, I need to take my shoes off in awe and worship. I do not presume to know what Jesus's solitude in the Garden of Gethsemane was like. I can only know what the Scriptures tell me.

But I do know His time there with God was profound and epic.

That night after what we call "the Last Supper," He went with His disciples to the Garden of Gethsemane. The Scripture tells us it was His "habit" to go there. It was a place of refuge and quiet for Him. Maybe it was a garden that belonged to friends. Or a garden open to all due to the Passover festivities. It contained olive trees and an olive press.

How fitting that it would be a garden of olive trees, as olives have to be crushed to extract their oil —Jesus would be crushed for us.

As He went to the Garden of Gethsemane, a curtain closed. He left the others—the disciples, the crowds, the noise—behind. (He did take His three closest friends a little farther with Him and told them, "My soul is deeply grieved to the point of death; remain here and keep watch" [Mark 14:34]. He told them to pray lest they fall into temptation. Then He went deeper into the garden by Himself.) He wanted to talk to His Father—alone. His prayer was earnest. Fervent. Perhaps He was horrified by the enormity of what lay ahead of Him. He was asking if there was any other way to accomplish God's plan. Surely God with His infinite power and wisdom could find another way. Any other way. He knew what a crucifixion was. He'd seen them. Probably many times.

Jesus wasn't looking for an escape. When the authorities came for Him, He said, "Do you think that I cannot appeal to My Father, and He will at once put at My disposal more than twelve legions of angels?" (Matt. 26:53). What we are seeing is His human side struggling with what would be in front of Him in just a matter of hours. We also see His divine nature willing to sacrifice Himself. Surely, there was temptation to disrupt God's plan. That's why He rebuked Peter in such a strong way when Peter said, "This shall never happen to you." Jesus replied, "Get behind me, Satan! You are a stumbling block to Me; for you are not setting your mind on God's interests, but man's" (16:22–23). Jesus's human side was tempted but His divine nature overruled.

But beyond the physical pain and humiliation awaiting Him was the fact that He knew all of humankind's sin would descend on Him on that cross. He was sinless, spotless. The perfect Lamb of God. How would He endure? He knew Isaiah's words: "But your iniquities have made a separation between you and your God, and your sins have hidden His face from you so that He does not hear" (Isa. 59:2). That must have been more terrifying than anything. He did not want to be separated from His Father—separated from the Trinity, His community. He prayed, "Father, if You are willing, remove this cup from Me; yet not My will, but Yours be done" (Luke 22:42).

Emotionally and spiritually drained, He then went back to His disciples and found them sleeping! They could not keep their heads up and eyes open. These were men who were used to fishing all night! Could they not hear His loud crying? Would they not be a little bit curious as to what was going on? He had already told them He was "deeply grieved, to the point of death" and asked them to "remain here and keep watch with Me" (Matt. 26:38). The enemy was working even there, making these men too drowsy to be praying with and for Jesus. His closest human companions did not have His back. I feel for those disciples. They'd just had dinner and their stomachs were full. And they'd had a busy couple of days.

We are told He prayed three times asking His Father that He not have "to drink this cup." And three times He surrendered to His Father's will, saying "not what I will, but what You will" (Mark 14:36).

Humanly, Jesus was truly alone. And He knew there was a crowd roused by the chief priests and scribes and the elders, accompanied by Judas, on their way to the garden to arrest Him.

The root of sin is self-will. "The essence of all sin is in the assertion of our will against the will of God."[2] Jesus fully surrendered to the will of His Father even though He struggled with it. Philippians 2:7 says He "emptied Himself, taking the form of a bond-servant."

We are told by the writer of Hebrews, "He offered up both prayers and supplications with loud crying and tears to the One able to save Him from death, and He was heard because of His piety" (Heb. 5:7). He appealed to His Father for some other way. And He was loud about it. He was crying. He was pleading.

He agonized so much in prayer that God sent an angel to strengthen Him. His Father did not ignore His Son. He wanted to comfort Him. God knew what His Son was facing.

I wonder what the angel did for him. Surely, the angel brought encouragement from the Father. Straight from the throne room of heaven, the angel might have assured Jesus that His Father heard Him. That His Father was listening and attentive. The angel may have reminded Him of His mission's purpose—not that He had forgotten. Jesus knew what lay ahead. He knew the cross was looming, but how easy it is to lose sight of your purpose when you are facing an overwhelming situation.

The angel would have spoken life over Him. Maybe the angel quoted psalms to Him. Maybe Psalm 89 or Psalm 91, reminding Him that God was a refuge and a fortress. That He was faithful. And that Jesus was His chosen, beloved Son. He might have told Jesus of God's justice and righteousness. That His hand was mighty. He might have said,

> I have chosen you and not rejected you.
> Do not fear, for I am with you;
> Do not anxiously look about you, for I am your God.
> I will strengthen you, surely I will help you,
> Surely I will uphold you with My righteous right
> hand. (Isa. 41:9–10)

Perhaps the angel gave Jesus a fresh vision of the "endgame"— His victory over death and hell and a vision of Him sitting victorious at His Father's right hand. Yes. The angel encouraged Jesus.

We are told that, "being in agony He was praying very fervently; and His sweat became like drops of blood, falling down upon the ground" (Luke 22:44). That is a condition called *hematidrosis*. It is caused when, in cases of severe fear or stress, capillaries, some of which are located around the sweat glands, burst and cause blood to exit the body through those glands.[3] It causes weakness and dehydration. Jesus needed that angel to strengthen Him!

We can say, "Oh, but Jesus wasn't really alone. He had an angel." And that is true. But we have supernatural help as well. As believers, we are never truly alone. We have the Holy Spirit inside of us. We are never as alone as Jesus was in His agony.

In His aloneness, Jesus surrendered. Totally. Gave it all, completely and without reservation. He abandoned Himself into the hands of God.

Abandoning Ourselves to God through Solitude

In the epigraph for this chapter, I quoted Henri Nouwen. I particularly love his insight that in solitude "Christ remodels us in his own image."[4] Isn't that a powerful motivation to be intentional about frequently dedicating time to "slip away" with God in solitude? We long to be more like Jesus and to be more deeply connected to Him. Now we know how. As we've seen, solitude can become a vital part of our lives, as it was for Jesus, during which we can cultivate a deeper intimacy with God. Let us cultivate solitude as Jesus did. Let us commit ourselves to frequently spending time alone with God. And when loneliness strikes, or major decisions loom ahead of us, or grief rolls over us, or we feel depleted and weary, or we thirst for a fresh taste of God's power and glory, let us choose to devote ourselves to solitude. While alone with Him, may we praise and worship Him, confess our sins to Him, be vulnerable and honest with Him, seek and submit to His will, and invite Him to minister to us.

Henri Nouwen also wrote,

> We enter into solitude first of all to meet our Lord and to be with Him and Him alone. Only in the context of grace can we face our sin; only in the place of healing do we dare to show our wounds; only with a single-minded attention to Christ can we give up our clinging fears and face our own true nature.[5]

May you, too, cultivate solitude.

But Jesus Himself would often slip away to the wilderness and pray.

Luke 5:16

9

The Choice to REACH

Everything can be taken from a man but one thing: the last of the human freedoms—to choose one's attitude in any given set of circumstances.

Viktor Frankl[1]

"I am alone. And overwhelmed," my friend Lori wrote in an email to me.

My daughter is a drinker. Several times she has told me she drinks too much and has decided to cut down. But she has not been able to. It has gotten worse. I have just come to the realization that she is an alcoholic. She swigs vodka in her car just so she can maintain her heavy work schedule. She has to have a drink in the morning to steady her hands in order to stir her coffee. My fear is that she will get into an accident and hurt someone or herself. She has a conceal-carry permit and a quick temper. That with alcohol is a bad combination. I am afraid for her.

I have no companion to talk this over with—no husband. No father—my father is in heaven. No brother and not a sister I can talk to. Perhaps there are those I could talk to but they might say my daughter needs to "pull herself up by her bootstraps and get a grip." Or they might overspiritualize it and quote Scriptures at me and my daughter. My pastor is fairly new so I hesitate to go to him yet. I feel so alone. I know God is with me but I don't feel His presence.

And yet I know God is providing help. I talked with my youngest daughter and she helped me decide who I needed to call. My daughter has a friend who truly loves her and will do anything for her—he was concerned and very glad I called. We talked, and he had seen my daughter's dependence on alcohol and resulting poor decisions. His concern and offer to help were a great comfort. God provided a psychiatrist who is a believer my daughter saw at least once for medication. Of course, he could not talk to me due to HIPPA laws but I could tell him what I saw and my concern. He told me who my daughter's counselor was. I called him. He also could not talk to me about my daughter due to HIPPA laws but again, I could tell him what I saw and my concerns. He was exactly what I needed.

The two of them told me of a residential rehabilitation facility. I called to see if they had room for my daughter. They did. When I called her, she said, "Mom, you've made a lot of phone calls." She told

me she was an alcoholic and had been for some time.
She was relieved and ready to get help. Even so, I feel
so alone in all of this. I know that in your Ruth Gra-
ham & Friends events you always addressed addic-
tion. Do you have any wisdom for me?

God had gone before my friend. While she felt alone, she wasn't. And Someone far better than a husband or sister was right with her. He had gone ahead, orchestrating everything for her and her daughter's good. "There is a friend who sticks closer than a brother" (Prov. 18:24). Because she chose to reach out to me, I was able to reassure her of God's presence with her, affirm the loving steps she had taken, and begin dialoguing with her about building a support team of her own.

I appreciate Lori's willingness to allow me to share her email with you. Though she'd felt lonely in dealing with her daughter's alcoholism, she'd taken quite a few wise steps by reaching out. In reaching out to God, to her daughter's friend, to professionals, to her other daughter, and to me, she'd not only discovered that she was no longer alone but she now understood that she'd never been alone at all. That God had been at work orchestrating everything for her and her daughter's good. Reaching out does that. It breaks the *illusion* of being alone. It opens the door to recovery from loneliness.

Recovery

In the years when my ministry, Ruth Graham & Friends, put on conferences that spoke to the many causes of brokenness often "hidden" or "masked" within the church, we included sessions on recovery from addiction and substance abuse. Over and over, often through whispered confessions and tears of relief, we heard from those who struggled in these areas that until the conference they'd never felt "safe" to reveal their struggle to other believers. Why? The deep shame they had felt and their intense fear of judgment had kept them paralyzed and silent.

Thanks to some great resources and wise teachers, I thought I had a fairly solid understanding of the foundations of addiction, and I was a strong advocate for the local church making itself a safe haven for recovery. But now, as I've done research for this book, I've discovered a link that had never before occurred to me: the link between addiction and loneliness.

Addiction of any kind involves the interplay of physical and mental health and is insidiously intertwined with loneliness. Loneliness and addiction are often interconnected and can lead to a vicious cycle—lonely people self-medicate to feel less lonely, but self-medication often results in greater feelings of loneliness. The cycle worsens from there. Why? "Because people who are lost to an active addiction unconsciously tend to alienate people around them, as the relationship with the substance becomes the primary relationship, excluding family and friends."[2] Can you see how the same could be true of loneliness? What if Lori had kept silent in her loneliness and not chosen to reach out? She would have then had a dark "secret" that her daughter was an alcoholic. In keeping her secret, she could have withdrawn and turned inward, suffering in silence, and then her illusion of being alone would have become her reality of being alone. But by her choice to reach out, she broke the power of her loneliness.

Think about this. Since loneliness can have such a negative impact on a person's brain chemistry (as we learned in chapter 5), it can give a person less self-control over behaviors, cravings, and emotions and therefore make them more susceptible to addictive behaviors. I'm not suggesting for a moment that we assume every lonely person is likely an addict but rather every addict is likely lonely. What a wake-up call this can be to the church. What an opportunity we have to *befriend* the addicted, to welcome them into our midst and surround them with the fellowship of believers. May we as the body of Christ learn to pave the road of recovery with our open arms and warm welcome.

What if we did the same for the lonely among us? What if the church did the same for us during lonely times?

I was intrigued by this theory of addiction given by Johann Hari in a TED Talk:

> Human beings have a natural and innate need to bond. And when we're happy and healthy we'll bond and connect with each other. But if you can't do that—because you're traumatized or isolated or beaten down by life—you will bond with something that will give you some sense of relief. Now that might be gambling, that might be pornography, that might be cocaine, that might be cannabis, but you will bond and connect with something because that's our nature, that's what we want as human beings.[3]

Did you notice his statement, "when we're happy and healthy we'll bond and connect with each other"? Well, as we discovered in the chapter "The Dark Side of Loneliness," when we are lonely, if we choose to stay there, we are neither happy nor healthy! That brings to mind the words of Jesus in Matthew 9:12, "But when Jesus heard this, He said, 'It is not those who are healthy who need a physician, but those who are sick.'" You and I, as those who suffer from loneliness, need healing from the Great Physician, just as an addict needs healing from addiction.

Do you think that might be an overstatement? Well, consider the following from an article that offered a list of the common feelings an addict has. I was incredibly surprised as I read it—not that an addict might feel this way but that the list matched so well the feelings loneliness so often brings with it. Take a look at this list and see if it captures some of your own feelings of loneliness.

- Feeling unable to connect with anyone—physically or emotionally.
- Feeling disconnected from others.
- Feeling sad there is no one available to talk with, be with, or understand you.
- Feeling that there is no one who cares.
- Feeling abandoned.
- Feeling as though no one wants to be with you.
- Feeling discontent.
- Feeling left out.
- Feeling hopeless.
- Fearing you will always feel this way.[4]

Do you recognize any of your own feelings in this list? I do! We have a lot in common, then, with those who suffer from addiction. And just as a person in recovery from addiction needs to come to the place of recognizing that they need help and reach out for it, so, too, must those of us who are lonely recognize we need to reach out for help.

Reaching Up and Reaching Out

If you've had any connections in your life to someone going through an addiction recovery program, you may be familiar with what is called a twelve-step program. It was first developed in the 1930s by the organizers of Alcoholics Anonymous and has been used and adapted since by any number of organizations to help those in recovery from various addictions or compulsions. I'm not planning to adapt it here for recovery from loneliness, but I mention it simply as an example of how helpful it can be to have a simple tool that helps one to remember and follow the steps or stages of making a major life change.

I've come up with a simple tool of my own that helps me remember five steps I can take when I am confronted by feelings of loneliness. These steps—these choices—remind me how I can work with God in transforming my loneliness into what I really long for: a deeper connection to God and to others. It is a simple acronym that spells REACH, and it reminds me of practical choices I can make to reach up to God and reach out to others when I feel lonely.

> R: **Recognize** the source, symptoms, and risks of your loneliness.
>
> E: **Express** your loneliness to God and another person.
>
> A: **Anticipate** that God will transform your loneliness into something positive and useful for His purposes.
>
> C: **Connect** with God (reach up) and others (reach out).

H: Honor God in your loneliness by making your loneliness sacred—make it holy by dedicating it to God.

I find REACH to be a specific, applicable, and memorable
tool. We'll be using it in each of the following chapters. In
fact, I've been invisibly using it all along in the organization
of this book. Chapters 1 through 5 were all about learning
to *recognize* the source, symptoms, and risks of our loneliness. Chapter 1 explored the universality of loneliness and
helped us recognize what we all long for: to be connected
to God and to others. Chapter 2 helped us recognize that
God sees us in our loneliness and is moved by love to intervene in our lives through it. Chapter 3 led us to recognize
the source of our loneliness and that we were designed for
connection and community with God and others. Chapter 4
illustrated the symptoms of loneliness and saw to it we
could see we share those symptoms with so many people
around the globe. Chapter 5 was all about recognizing the
dangerous risks of loneliness left unchecked. Together these
five chapters taught us to recognize and name our loneliness
for what it is, to identify the source of our loneliness, and
to acknowledge the toll it is taking, or could take, on our
lives and health.

We moved on from *recognize* to *express* in chapter 6 as
we discovered the critically important step of choosing to
partner with God in our loneliness and inviting Him into our
loneliness so He can transform it. That invitation needs to be
expressed to God. And here in chapter 9, as we explore the
choice to reach up and reach out, we are learning to express
our loneliness to at least one other person, following Lori's
example, for by breaking our silence we are also beginning

to break through our loneliness. I discovered this lesson for myself when I went off to Gordon College.

Expressing Our Loneliness to Another

You will recall my story of being sent off at age fifteen to boarding school in New York. As I revealed, I was miserably lonely and clung only to God until at last He brought a dear friend into my life who then became my roommate. She and God were my companions as I completed that year. What happened next is still a bit of a mystery to me, but somehow between my parents, the administrators, and myself, the decision was made that rather than attend one final year of high school, I'd go straight on to Gordon College at the age of sixteen.

Just as I had the year before, I found myself in September arriving on another campus I'd never even visited, not knowing a single soul. I'm sure I was the youngest student there. I had no idea what I wanted to study or what I wanted to do with my life, and I felt clueless about how to navigate college. Gordon was academically rigorous, so I threw myself into my studies and just held on for dear life. It was sink or swim, so I started swimming. Again, I was desperately lonely. I greatly missed my roommate from the year before as we'd grown close. But this time I had something new going for me—the experience of the year before. I reached up to God by stepping into the same habits of turning daily to prayer and the Bible for comfort. And, largely because of the habit I'd grown into the year before, I took the chance of reaching out to my new roommate. I told her I was lonely. I was transparent about how much I missed my best friend, and soon we were sharing our confidences. We, too, became best friends, and that friendship got me through my first year at Gordon. Her family just about adopted me. Their love for me was so effusive! We still remain close. That didn't ease all my struggle, of course. I was young, southern, Billy Graham's daughter, and not really qualified to be there. I did not fit in well. But my roommate and her family and friends all accepted me, and that made all the difference.

As you consider the loneliness you are now experiencing, I encourage you to reach up to God by inviting Him to transform your loneliness into something positive, and to reach out to at least one person, entrusting him or her with the fact that you are feeling lonely. Seek God's wisdom for who that someone might be. A family member? Someone from your church or small group? Someone at work? If you can't find anyone with whom you feel safe with that information, then consider a pastor or a counselor. But don't try to go it alone. Reach out!

To this point, then, we've worked our way through two choices: *R* for recognize and *E* for express. Next comes *A*, the choice to *anticipate*. Anticipation is a powerful attitude. Let's explore this by taking a look at the well-known story of Abraham and Isaac.

Abraham's Anticipation

Abraham was an old man but still strong and very determined. He walked slowly up the mountain with a heavy heart. God had told him, "Take now your son, your only son, whom you love, Isaac, and go to the land of Moriah, and offer him there as a burnt offering on one of the mountains of which I will tell you" (Gen. 22:2). Abraham obeyed. He got up the very next morning and started out with his son for the place God would show him.

He must have had questions. We know Abraham to be a man of great faith. But he was human. He had prayed and waited for this child year after year. Isaac was his joy—his promise from God—the way God was going to fulfill all the promises He had made. Why would God ask him to kill his only son, the one God had promised and delivered as part of the covenant? How could God fulfill those wonderful promises if Isaac was sacrificed on an altar? Had he even heard God correctly? Was God really serious? This was out of character for God—He condemned human sacrifice! For, even in His instructions, God had acknowledged this was Abraham's only son and that he was dear to his heart. Yet His instructions were clear. So, step by heavy step, Abraham lumbered up the mountain with Isaac walking beside him.

I cannot begin to imagine the heaviness in Abraham's heart. There wasn't anyone he could talk to about it. I am sure he didn't tell Sarah—she would have done all in her power to stop him. He hadn't told Isaac. He couldn't. He was alone on that journey. Alone in his thoughts and questions. Terribly alone. But Abraham was obedient to God. And he believed God would keep His promises. Even so, this was horribly difficult.

Isaac was carrying the wood for the sacrifice for worship. At some point Isaac looked around and saw his father's knife and the fire. But no animal for the sacrifice. Isaac turned to his father and asked, "Where is the lamb for the burnt offering?" (v. 7).

Isaac's innocent and trusting question must have nearly broken Abraham's heart. Abraham told Isaac, "God will provide for Himself the lamb for the burnt offering, my son" (v. 8).

Abraham believed. I love what James wrote about Abraham in the New Testament: "'And Abraham believed God, and it was reckoned to him as righteousness,' and he was called a friend of God" (James 2:23). I'm sure, as Abraham climbed, he thought about how, humanly speaking, it would have been impossible for him and Sarah to have conceived Isaac at such a late age, but they had. If God could do that, then surely God could do other miracles. Abraham was "fully assured that what God had promised, He was able also to perform" (Rom. 4:21). *Fully assured.* That is a powerful description of faith. Have you ever noticed what Hebrews 11:19 says about Abraham during this ordeal? "He considered that God is able to raise people even from the dead." Yes, surely Abraham must have wondered what God was up to, but as he wondered, he pondered what God *could* do. He chose to *anticipate* what God might do.

Slowly he walked on, alone with his questions, alone in his thoughts. Did he talk to God as he trudged up that hill? He couldn't have talked aloud because Isaac would have overheard, but maybe silently he did. If it had been me, I would have tried to talk God out of it. I would have been angry with God, questioned God, argued with God. But as far as we know Abraham did none of those things. He didn't know *how* God would fulfill the promise if Isaac were to die on that altar but knew God *would* fulfill that promise. He was sure of it. For by now Abraham had walked with God for a long time. They were friends.

Still, friends or not, when something life-shaking happens and you don't understand God, you can find yourself in a very lonely place.

By the very fact that Abraham kept on climbing, I believe with each step Abraham worshiped as he walked up that hill. His trust was a form of worship. And even more than that, I believe there was an anticipation in Abraham to see what God was going to do. After all, we know he considered that God was able to raise people from the dead. As difficult as it was, he knew God would fulfill His promise; he just didn't know how.

I suggest that is how you and I can respond when confronted with deep and painful loneliness: with anticipation. We can worship God by putting one foot in front of the other on our long journey of climbing our mountain, not knowing *how* God is at work but fully assured that He *is* at work for our good and His purposes. After all, this is the God who raises the dead! This is the God who provided the perfect Lamb as the sacrifice.

During Jesus's Sermon on the Mount, He said,

> Ask, and it will be given to you; seek, and you will find; knock, and it will be opened to you. For everyone who asks receives, and he who seeks finds, and to him who knocks it will be opened. Or what man is there among you who, when his son asks for a loaf, will give him a stone? Or if he asks for a fish, he will not give him a snake, will he? If you then, being evil, know how to give good gifts to your children, how much more will your Father who is in heaven give what is good to those who ask Him! (Matt. 7:7–11)

Do you believe that? Do you trust that God is eager to "give good gifts" to His children? That trust can lead you to an attitude of anticipation. As I look back now on my lonely year in the New York high school and my lonely year at Gordon, I can't help but wonder if God was intentionally placing me in schools He knew would be far outside of my comfort zone so that my discomfort would push me into a new zone entirely. A zone of dependence on Him. A zone of anticipating what good gifts He had in store for me next.

You are lonely. What might God have in store for you next? Pray that God will fill you, now, with anticipation for what He is up to. If you need some help arriving at that choice to anticipate, then I believe the next chapter may help you get there. But first, let's take a look at the final two letters in our REACH acronym.

The Choice to Connect

Because I had no clue about what I wanted out of college, I married at the young age of eighteen to a man a bit older than I was. I was eager to have my own home and family. We lived in Valley Forge, Pennsylvania, some miles from his family. He worked for his father in Philadelphia, and we often had family gatherings. Naively, I believed now that I was married I'd never be lonely again. But married life quickly taught me otherwise. My husband was a very busy businessman who threw himself into his work. I'd always looked forward to raising a family, so we wasted no time in trying to start one, but it took four years before that became a reality. Then I threw myself into mothering. By the time I was in my late twenties we had three children.

Then came a major change. My husband was interested in raising horses, so we bought some acreage outside of Argyle,

Texas, where we could raise both horses and children. With my husband gone so often for long hours at work, living in a new state, looking for a new church, missing my friends in Philadelphia, being far from my family, and trying to cope with a whole different lifestyle, I felt very isolated. I quickly realized I needed to make some connections.

I'll be forever grateful that God led me to Bible Study Fellowship (BSF). It was in Dallas, which was a one-hour drive from my home, but that drive was so worth it. BSF became my lifeline. First, the time spent in the Bible connected me directly to the heart of God. I drank it in and felt my soul being deeply nourished. But BSF also connected me to the fellowship of other women who loved God and were eager to extend their friendship. I no longer felt alone, and I knew I was also contributing to their lives spiritually and relationally.

Then God surprised me with an added bonus. I learned that a childhood friend, Kathy Burns, lived in Dallas as well. Ours was a remarkable three-generation relationship. Her grandmother and my grandmother had been friends. Our mothers were also friends, so I first "met" her family while still in the crib! Then she and I became friends as children. Now we reunited, and our friendship blossomed. I was also able to reconnect with her family, which brought me great joy. I felt like I was among family whenever we visited. Even more remarkable: our daughters have since become friends, making it now a four-generation friendship. They are all still dear to me, and even now Kathy and I connect every day to keep each other accountable to exercise.

My Texas experience demonstrated to me the importance of staying connected with God and with others. I learned that both of those relationships required a commitment of time and energy, and that God richly rewarded that investment. But it never would have happened had I stayed isolated at home with my three children. It required a deliberate choice to reach up to God and to reach out to others. That is what the C in REACH is all about—the choice to *connect* with God and with others.

I urge you, no matter how discouraged you feel in your loneliness, no matter how drained or exhausted you are, no matter how hopeless it seems to extend yourself in some way, make the choice now—even if you don't yet know how or where—to connect with God and connect with others. The rest of this book is designed to inspire and equip you in those two critically important connections. I pray you will find a fresh perspective that will engage and energize you to do just that.

Honor God

The final choice in REACH is to *honor* God in your loneliness by making your loneliness sacred. That phrase may sound unfamiliar and even strange to you. To make something sacred or holy means to dedicate it to God. To invite God to put it to His use. It doesn't mean to change it, transform it, or ignore it but to wholeheartedly dedicate it to God. Making something sacred is an act of the will. It means letting go of it and entrusting it to God's good use as He sees fit. I'm not for one minute going to suggest that it's easy. Or that it's necessarily fast. But I am going to declare that it's *possible* because it is a choice we can make, regardless of the emotions we feel.

160

As you can see, this chapter has been all about choices you can make *in* your loneliness, because often the reality is the circumstances that lead to our loneliness are beyond our control. Our choices, though—our attitudes—are within our power to change. REACH for God in your loneliness.

> **How much more will your Father who is in heaven give what is good to those who ask Him!**
>
> Matthew 7:11

10

The Affirmation
of Being Chosen

Every page of the New Testament tells us about the deep
friendship and love that Jesus feels for us.

Emilie Griffen[1]

I have a grandson who was born with significant challenges.
His esophagus was not connected to his stomach; consequently they inserted a G-tube. After many months and four
major surgeries, he was finally released from the hospital. In
no time at all they realized his trachea was collapsing, and
he had to have a trach put in so he could breathe. Back into
the hospital he went for more major surgeries. He spent the
first one hundred and sixty-one days of his life in children's
hospitals both in Wilmington and Philadelphia. Needless
to say, he got off to a shaky start. When he was nine the
trach was removed and repaired—with more surgery. He was
eleven before he was finally able to be weaned off the G-tube.

I so admire my daughter Windsor and her husband, Todd.
If you look up "mama bear" in the dictionary you will find

her picture! She and her husband advocated for that little guy each step of the way. And they had an eighteen-month-old daughter at home at the time he was born! It was not easy. It was downright hard, and some days they just weren't sure they would survive.

Often having a special needs child dooms a marriage. My hat is off to Windsor and Todd. They stuck together through thick and thin. There were days they wanted to quit but chose to stay, and today they have a solid, happy marriage where they truly are each other's best friend. I so admire my son-in-law, who quit his cherished photography business to work for UPS in order to have the insurance needed for his son. He did it cheerfully and with enthusiasm, as he does everything. They have a great family.

They have always made every effort to treat my grandson just like any boy. As a baby, they would take him on walks and hikes even though they had to lug a heavy emergency bag with them. They needed nursing care in their home twenty-four hours a day—and it was tight quarters. They were often stared at, especially in restaurants where he sometimes would have a gagging episode. But they just kept right on going. When they took him to the beach, I remember feeling so sad for him as he watched the others splash in the waves while he could only watch from the shore and play in the sand. But he didn't complain, and they didn't feel sorry for themselves. It was their life.

He has a huge persona with a million-dollar smile, blue eyes, and dimples. He has a strong personality and never gives up. His life is different from other kids. He tries to keep up—even trying to play tag football with the big boys. But he will always be different. He is and will remain considerably shorter than other boys his age. I know he will find his niche and do well, in part because his parents have given him as good and normal a life as possible.

When asked if he gets lonely because he is different, he will shrug his shoulders and say, "Sometimes." But when pressed he will acknowledge the loneliness of the weeks spent in the hospital. He played his video games to keep himself company.

He says he hates being short. "Everyone towers over me, but I find a way around them." It is frustrating to him. Sometimes at recess no one plays with him, so he has to find something he can do on his own. But he does not feel sorry for himself.

There is a character in the Bible who was known to be quite short as well: Zacchaeus. He, like my grandson, was often excluded by others, though the reasons were far different. He lived and worked in Jericho as the chief tax collector. The Romans farmed out tax collection to Jewish people willing to take the job, and each tax collector could extort more than his fair share from those in his jurisdiction. Tax collectors were notoriously crooked and overtaxed the people to gain personal wealth. They made life miserable. They were hated. Zacchaeus was not a popular figure. He was ostracized by the Jewish community, his own people. I expect that he was a very lonely man.

Jericho had a rich history. This was the town Joshua and the Israelites marched around seven times, then blew their trumpets and the walls "came tumbling down." It was a very important town as it sat at a crossroads and controlled ancient trade routes from the east. Once across the Jordan River, one route went toward Bethel and Shechem in the north, another went west toward Jerusalem, and yet a third went south to Hebron. Jericho controlled the hill country of Palestine. Many Jewish people came through Jericho on their way to Jerusalem to avoid Samaria because they despised the Samaritans and did not want to be defiled on their way to the temple.

Zacchaeus lived up to the reputation of tax collectors. And with the trade routes going through the Jericho region, he made a killing. He was rich and he was loathed. Being short, he may have also had a Napoleon complex, which would have endeared him to no one. Because of his position he got the gossip before most, and one day he heard that a new rabbi who was drawing big crowds, Jesus, was coming to Jericho. Oh boy! That was the ticket to have. Zacchaeus had to see what was going on.

But the crowds were so large he couldn't get close to Jesus. And no one was going to make way for the chief tax collector. Perhaps, as he tried to get close, he was pushed farther back by those who didn't like him. In frustration, he realized the only way he would be able to see Jesus was to climb a nearby sycamore tree. He'd probably climbed many as a boy. So up he went.

And there Jesus was—right beneath him. Talk about a front-row seat! Zacchaeus could see and hear Jesus without any obstruction. Then something unexpected happened. Jesus stopped right in front of the sycamore tree. He looked up at the hated tax collector and said, "Zacchaeus, hurry and come down, for today I must stay at your house" (Luke 19:5).

Zacchaeus was absolutely amazed that Jesus not only saw him but knew his name! He climbed right down and "received Him gladly" (v. 6). He was in awe to have the "celebrity of the day" notice him and, better yet, to have Him want to come home with him. What an honor.

You can imagine how the crowd responded. Eyebrows no doubt shot up. Jaws dropped open. Of all the people in town whom Jesus might have honored with a visit, he was choosing Zacchaeus? The miserable thieving tax collector? The crowd grumbled about Jesus going to a sinner's house. How dare He!

But what happens next is a surprise. Something began to happen inside Zacchaeus.

Zacchaeus stopped, turned to Jesus, and said, "Behold, Lord, half of my possessions I will give to the poor, and if I have defrauded anyone of anything, I will give back four times as much" (v. 8).

Such is the power of the friendship of Jesus. Jesus *chose* him. He stopped and called him by name. He wanted to stay at his home. No conditions—Jesus was offering His friendship to Zacchaeus exactly as he was. What was it like for a despised man, marginalized and condemned by the crowd, to be noticed and singled out and chosen by Jesus? Usually, if anyone paid attention to him, it was negative attention.

Like the Grinch, Zacchaeus's heart grew three sizes that day! Zacchaeus recognized Jesus as Lord—not just as a rabbi. He was Lord. Over Zacchaeus and his money. Zacchaeus was so overwhelmed he decided to make things right—even giving back four times as much as he'd taken. That decision was costly to Zacchaeus.

Jesus then announced, "Today salvation has come to this house, because he, too, is a son of Abraham. For the Son of Man has come to seek and to save that which was lost" (vv. 9–10).

Jesus saw his changed heart and made the declaration that Zacchaeus was part of God's family. He belonged. And Jesus valued him by vouching for him in front of all the townspeople.

Chosen as Friends

We are all Zacchaeus. Undeserving. Marred by our sin. "Small" compared to the greatness of God. And lonely—longing to be seen, to be chosen, to be known, to belong, and to be valued. And just as Jesus did for Zacchaeus, Jesus sees us, chooses us, knows us, claims us as belonging to His family, and values us.

I believe there is no better news for the lonely than that!

In the previous chapter we discussed how we all have the choice—the opportunity—to reach up to connect with God and to reach out to connect with others. In this and the remaining chapters we'll be exploring *how*, as lonely people, to do that effectively in such a way that our loneliness is transformed into a deeper connection with God and others.

Zacchaeus's experience with Jesus paints the picture for us. Notice that he didn't reach up or reach out until Jesus reached *into* him. Jesus saw him, then chose him, then knew him. And because of that, Zacchaeus was transformed.

You and I need to wrap our hearts and minds around this process—this truth, this experience—so that our hearts, too, are deeply touched and transformed like Zacchaeus's. And to help us do that, we have the words of Jesus on His final night on earth before He was crucified.

After Jesus and the disciples had finished the Last Supper, just before going to the Garden of Gethsemane, Jesus taught His disciples one last time. John captures it all in John 13 through 17. If ever, during a time of solitude, you want to better know the heart of Jesus toward you, I encourage you to read those five chapters in one sitting. He had so much He wanted them to know and remember. Every word is precious.

I'm always moved by how John begins Jesus's farewell discourse.

> Now before the Feast of the Passover, Jesus, knowing that His hour had come that He would depart out of this world to the Father, having loved His own who were in the world, He loved them to the end. (John 13:1)

Yes. He loved them to the end. He loves *us* just as much. And among His words of love are three verses that I believe have a special meaning to the lonely. They certainly minister to me in my loneliness. They also have a profound effect on how you and I relate to Jesus and on how you and I befriend others. Let's focus on them one at a time.

Jesus Calls You His Friend

In my mind's eye, before speaking these words Jesus looked around the room and into the eyes of His disciples. Picture Him looking into your eyes as He says this: "No longer do I call you slaves, for the slave does not know what his master is doing; but I have called you friends, for all things that I have heard from My Father I have made known to you" (John 15:15).

No matter how lonely you may ever feel, the fact is you have a Friend in Jesus. The Son of God, who was with God from the beginning, who together with the Father created all there is, calls you His personal friend. A Friend who left heaven and came to earth for you. A Friend who spent His earthly life revealing God to you. A Friend who died for you so that He could present you before the Father as holy and blameless, so that you could spend eternity enjoying your friendship with God. A Friend who sent the Holy Spirit to dwell in you.

He sees you as He saw Zacchaeus—just as you are, flaws and all—and still He calls you by name. He loves your company. And He is coming to your place to stay. It's personal with Him. He's moving in! Because of His friendship you are never alone. And because of His friendship you will never be the same. "Therefore if anyone is in Christ, he is a new creature; the old things passed away; behold, new things have come" (2 Cor. 5:17). His friendship transforms you just as it did Zacchaeus.

"Only when we have confronted the reality of our loneliness can we grasp the overwhelming significance of what Jesus offers us: transforming friendship with God."[2] In calling you His friend, Jesus is giving you unconditional friendship, loving you just as you are, warts and all.

Jesus Chose You

In His very next breath, Jesus said this: "You did not choose Me but I chose you, and appointed you that you would go and bear fruit" (John 15:16).

Why did He choose us? "He chose us in Him before the foundation of the world, that we would be holy and blameless before Him" (Eph. 1:4). Do you remember why you are lonely in the first place, as we discussed in chapter 3? Because you were designed for community and connection with God and others, and that connection was broken by sin. Now you've been chosen so that Jesus can present you as holy and blameless to the Father and your fellowship with God can be restored, now and for all eternity.

170

As one who is chosen by Jesus you've been given a job to do: to bear fruit. In John 15:1–5, Jesus explained that He is the vine and we are the branches. As long as we "abide" in Him—stay connected to Him and dwell in Him and draw our very sustenance from Him—then we will bear fruit. To bear fruit is to grow into who God created us to be, to draw others to Jesus, to make disciples. It is also to bear the fruit of the Spirit, which is "love, joy, peace, patience, kindness, goodness, faithfulness, gentleness, self-control" (Gal. 5:22–23).

And because you are chosen, you are part of God's family. "But you are a chosen race, a royal priesthood, a holy nation, a people for God's own possession, so that you may proclaim the excellencies of Him who has called you out of darkness into His marvelous light" (1 Pet. 2:9). Just as Jesus declared to crowds at Jericho that Zacchaeus belonged to His family, so, too, you belong to His family—His holy nation. You've been made holy!

This quote expresses that part of ourselves that will never be the same: "God longs to meet us in the depths of our being, especially in those broken parts we consider unacceptable and sinful."[3]

In choosing you to bear fruit, He—as the vine—is pouring into you His love and mercy and grace and holiness so they fill you up and overflow as fruit in your life (the fruit of the Spirit), attracting others to Jesus (making disciples).

Jesus Calls You to Love Others

And now we come to the third verse Jesus spoke on His last night that I believe has special meaning to the lonely: "This I command you, that you love one another" (John 15:17).

171

This verse has a profound impact on how you befriend others—on the kind of friend you will be—and that, perhaps more than anything else, will transform your loneliness into deep, rich, and satisfying relationships with others. "We have come to know and have believed the love which God has for us. God is love, and the one who abides in love abides in God, and God abides in him" (1 John 4:16). When we love others, we are representing God to them. We are meeting their needs. We are giving of ourselves. We are meeting the greatest need anyone has.

Mother Teresa wrote, "We can cure physical diseases with medicine, but the only cure for loneliness, despair, and hopelessness is love. There are many in the world who are dying for a piece of bread but there are many more dying for a little love."[4]

In calling you to love others Jesus is trusting you to feed and nourish and bless others, and that will create the kind of connection to others that satisfies loneliness.

Befriend, Choose, and Love Others

Consider for a moment the disciples whom Jesus chose to travel with Him, learn from Him, and then begin His church. Like Zacchaeus, like us, they were far from perfect. One was a tax collector. One was a doubter. One was a betrayer. One was a denier. Two often sought to be important. They were all a little slow to understand. They didn't always "get" what He taught, but He handpicked them to be His friends. He knew their flaws. He understood them. He taught them. He died for them. He forgave them. In other words, He loved them.

In His relationships with them He was modeling for us how we are to relate to others. Do you recall what we learned in chapter 4—that this world is filled with lonely people? Remember that it's likely, whenever you are in a group of people, about half of them have the well-kept secret that they are lonely, just as you are. They need you. You need each other! Rather than assuming others are what they appear to be—confident, connected, and content—assume they long for you to choose them as your friend and to accept them as they are. Reach out to them, flaws and all.

This makes me think of Peter.

The disciples were exhilarated but exhausted. They had divided a crowd of five thousand–plus into groups of fifty to sit on the grass, then distributed two fish and five loaves of bread to all those folks. Then they gathered the leftovers. And that was after a long day of Jesus teaching. They were spent. Jesus told them to get into the boat and head across the Sea of Galilee. He'd meet them on the other side.

They climbed into the boat and started rowing. It wasn't long before a storm arose. The Sea of Galilee is noted for its sudden storms, because cold air from the mountains sweeps through the ravines and gorges to meet the warm air of the valley. But these were experienced fishermen who knew the sea well. They didn't turn back but rowed on, thinking they could manage it. But their weariness and the strength of the storm put fear in their hearts. Storms will do that to us.

Jesus was alone praying. He, too, was tired and weary. He needed to talk with His Father. But He knew of their distress and left His praying to head toward them. He loved them so much that in the early hours of the morning He quit His own time with God to go to them. By this point the disciples had been struggling a long time. Suddenly, they saw Jesus coming toward them, walking on the water.

They couldn't believe their eyes. They thought this must be a ghost and were terrified. So terrified that "they cried out in fear" (Matt. 14:26). Jesus, knowing and understanding their terror, immediately called out to them, "Take courage, it is I; do not be afraid" (v. 27).

You've got to love Peter. He's always so bold, so quick to respond, so spontaneous. He shocked them all by shouting back, "Lord, if it is You, command me to come to You on the water" (v. 28).

Notice that he still isn't quite sure if it is the Lord. What made him say that? Was it the euphoria of the impossibility he was seeing right before his eyes? Was it excitement? Adrenaline? Did he just want confirmation it was the Lord? Probably a wild combination of all that and more.

"Come!" Jesus said.

And Peter got out of the boat. Wow! He just got out of the boat. And to his own amazement and that of the other disciples, he began to walk on the water too! He walked toward Jesus. He was moving in the right direction. But then "seeing the wind, he became frightened" and took his eyes off of Jesus. He began to sink. He did what we all would have done—he cried out "Lord, save me!" (v. 30).

I love that! Peter's prayer was immediate. It was focused. It was clear. He just hollered for help. The Lord immediately "stretched out His hand and took hold of him" (v. 31).

That's what I want you to see here. I want you to see Jesus stretching out His hand and grabbing Peter and not letting go. Pulling him up. Helping him into the boat. Both of them soaked through. Jesus is always reaching for us. In spite of our lack of faith. In spite of our sin. In spite of our failure. In spite of the fact that we take our eyes off of Him. He reaches out and takes hold of us.

"This is My commandment, that you love one another, just as I have loved you" (John 15:12). Can you see yourself reaching, like Jesus, for someone else who is floundering, sinking in loneliness? That's what Jesus would have you do. Just as He reaches for you, you can reach out to someone else. Take the risk. Look around you—at work, in the neighborhood, at the coffee shop, in the salon, at the grocery store. Choose someone to call your friend. Just try it. Be willing to accept them as they are, unconditionally, flaws and all. Identify with them in some way. You are not going to do it perfectly. That's not what Jesus asks of you. By stretching out your hand you could be the hand of Jesus to another lonely soul.

Do you remember from chapter 5 how dangerous loneliness can be to our health? Then consider this:

> The good news is that friendships reduce the risk of mortality or developing certain diseases and can speed recovery in those who fall ill. Moreover, simply reaching out to lonely people can jump-start the process of getting them to engage with neighbors and peers, according to Robin Caruso of CareMore Health.[5]

Did you catch it? "Simply reaching out." Will it give you the deep connection you are longing for? Maybe. Maybe not. But it can "jump-start the process" for you both! When Jesus tells us to love one another, He's not commanding that only because it's good for the other person but because it is good for us as well.

Cultivating Connections

I admire my former husband. He has turned his loneliness into visiting people in nursing homes. He has "regulars." He knows what candy they like and makes sure they get some. If he sees an article in the newspaper or a magazine that might interest them, he cuts it out and takes it to them. These are simple gestures that make a person feel seen and valued. He is always thinking of others. I am grateful for his example. He is reaching out.

The first step in making a friend is to be a friend. Be friendly. Smile and introduce yourself. When you are around a genuinely honest, thoughtful person, it makes you feel good. It's contagious. Their authenticity makes you want to be authentic. You don't have to watch your words. You are free to be yourself. That's what makes for a great foundation for friendship—when you are both authentic. Be real. Don't pretend to be something you are not. People can see through that. No one enjoys a fake. Simply listen to what they are saying and asking. Then ask follow-up questions.

My children smile when they know I am going to the grocery store because they know I'll speak to everyone there. It's my social hour! I know the clerks by name. I care about them. One of the store managers is a lovely lady named Lisa. She never meets a stranger, and each of her customers is special to her. We know she truly cares about us as her customers and as her friends. She always has a word of encouragement and a smile. She calls everyone "honey." I think she sets the tone for the whole store. There is a bigger, fancier store nearer my home, but I prefer this one because of the people. Maybe it is my "Cheers."

Have any of those grocery store relationships become deep friendships for me? No. Not so far. But when you chat with someone week after week with the intentional purpose of showing God's love, it's amazing how much you will learn about one another's lives over time. Especially if you sprinkle your small talk with unobtrusive questions and some self-disclosure. You start sharing about your family and about milestone events. About trips and weddings and funerals. About someone in the hospital. About church. Mother Teresa was right when she said that people are dying for a little love. What for you might be only "small talk" might be for the other person the only time anyone has shown interest in their life for days or weeks or far longer. You may be nourishing a soul in a way you'll never know.

How do we nudge a pleasant acquaintance into deeper friendship? How do we develop meaningful "heart friends"? Well, that takes time. I read somewhere that friendships take over two hundred hours to develop. I don't know if that is true, but I do know a good friendship takes time. Oh, there are some in which you'll feel an immediate connection, but those are rare. Most good friendships are developed over time and shared experiences where you build connections. Some of my best friendships were made when we had small children at the same time. Then as that experience changed, we went on to connect around church or school or jobs. We never let our friendships go. Even through moves, job changes, and divorce.

Many times, you have to make the first move to grow a relationship from an acquaintance to a friend. As I am more of an introvert, I relate to friends easily but it is hard for me to be the one to reach out. I have to be intentional and invest energy to do it, but I know that is what it takes. You might want to choose a casual acquaintance whom you really enjoy and test the waters in exploring a slightly deeper connection. Take the first step. Invite them to have a cup of coffee at your favorite coffee shop. Maybe make up a list of questions in your mind to have at the ready in case things lag a bit—not that this should be an inquisition! Ask how many children they have, or where they live in town. Where do they buy groceries? What are they reading? Just icebreaker questions. And soon you will be in a good conversation and making plans to see each other again!

We are seen by Jesus and uniquely chosen to be His friend, with our flaws and faults as well as our strengths, and we are wanted and enjoyed. We matter. Once we know and experience this with Jesus we can reach out to others in such a way that we communicate we choose them in the same way.

As you think about what it means to you that Jesus chose you, and how much you are affirmed when someone else chooses you as their friend, think about these words of Jesus: "In everything, therefore, treat people the same way you want them to treat you" (Matt. 7:12). Becoming one who chooses to give others attention is the perfect way to (1) follow the command of Jesus to treat others as you want to be treated, (2) make new friends and therefore be less lonely, and (3) model for others the love of Jesus. In this way, you are partnering with God in converting your desire to be chosen into the practice of choosing others. That is transformation!

REACH

As I mentioned in the previous chapter, as a way to help you remember and apply these principles to your life, each of our remaining chapters will end with the REACH exercise.

R—Recognize that in your loneliness, one of the things you long for is to feel personally affirmed, to be chosen by someone.

E—Express your need for affirmation to God in prayer right now.

A—Anticipate that God will transform your desire for affirmation, for being chosen, into the motivation to affirm others.

C—Connect with God (reach up) by meditating on His words, "I chose you." Praise Him for His affirmation and affirm Him by celebrating that you have chosen Him to be your Lord. Connect with others (reach out) by choosing one other person over the next week to affirm in some concrete way.

H—Honor God in your loneliness through making your need for affirmation sacred by dedicating it to God and for His purposes.

I have called you friends . . . I chose you . . .
love one another.

John 15:15–17

11

The Comfort of Being Known

The foundation of courage is vulnerability . . . we have to
show up and put ourselves out there.

Brené Brown[1]

Alison Owen-Jones was wrestling with a dilemma.

One day while walking her dog at the city park in her
hometown of Cardiff, UK, she noticed an elderly man sitting alone on a nearby park bench. He seemed to be people
watching. Another woman walking her dog strolled by him.
The elderly man looked up but the dog walker quickly passed
by without acknowledging him. Not far behind came two
young men jogging side by side. They passed the man apparently without noticing him. But Alison noticed. She was a
warm, friendly woman who enjoyed saying hello and meeting new people. Alison continued walking her dog but she
kept her eye on the older gentleman. Forty minutes passed,
and Alison couldn't help but feel sad that not a single person
acknowledged him. Not a couple pushing a stroller (called
pushchairs in the UK), other joggers, a teenager wearing his

headphones, or a woman taking a stroll. It was as if the old man was invisible.

Alison thought about walking over, sitting next to him, and chatting, but said, "There was some of that British reserve that made me think he may think me weird if I sat next to him." So she didn't. But she did think, *Wouldn't it be nice if there was a simple way to let people know you're open to a chat?*

This spawned an idea in Alison. What if she came to the park with a laminated sign and tied it to a bench? The sign could say, "Happy to chat bench. Sit here if you don't mind someone stopping to say hello." Would anyone sit down? To find out, she made a sign and sat next to it. She nodded and smiled at passersby. "All of a sudden, you're not invisible anymore," says Alison. She was delighted when people began noticing, smiling and nodding, and occasionally even sitting down next to her. Conversations ensued.

Alison loved her new self-made role and began frequenting the park with her sign. Somehow social media took notice and word spread about Alison's chat bench. The idea caught on and was replicated in another town in the UK, and then another and another. Soon Alison was besieged by communications from others interested in setting up their own chat benches. Eventually a charity named Senior Citizen Liaison Team took over handling the requests for information. People from Canada, the United States, Australia, Switzerland, and Ukraine have contacted the charity, all interested in copying the idea to get people talking.[2]

Isn't it amazing how one small innovative step by a woman in England has mushroomed into a global movement? Imagine: today, there are people sitting on chat benches around the world doing their part in relieving some of the loneliness in our world. I believe it's because Alison tapped into one of the core needs we humans all share, the longing to be known. I'm not suggesting that chat benches are for everyone. There is no "one size fits all" remedy for the lack of connection many of us feel. But whether we are sitting on chat benches or finding another way to step out, it seems our mutual longing to be known and to know others makes us all want to applaud the Alisons of the world.

Longing to Be Known

Do you remember the UCLA Loneliness Scale in appendix B we discussed in chapter 4? Consider again four of the questions on that survey. Where do you rate yourself, on a scale of 1 to 4 (1 = never, 4 = often)?

- How often do you feel that there is no one you can turn to?
- How often do you feel that you are no longer close to anyone?
- How often do you feel that your relationships with others are not meaningful?
- How often do you feel that no one really knows you well?

All four of these questions tap into our universal need to know others and be known by others and to experience intimacy, vulnerability, transparency, and closeness. Memoirist Melissa Febos wrote, "There are few experiences as powerful as articulating your vulnerability in the presence of another."[3] How long has it been since you've felt the power of a moment like that? Too long?

Of course, you and I realize moments like that don't just materialize out of the blue. And a chat bench isn't likely to create such a moment. (Though it can be a start!) In my experience, relationships need to grow into that level of sharing. We begin as strangers, move on to acquaintances, then advance to friends, all before arriving at a close friendship. Then within a close friendship we build up enough trust to test the waters a bit by revealing part of our deepest selves and nearly holding our breath to see if our transparency is met with genuine acceptance and understanding. And then, if that deep acceptance and understanding are found and reciprocated, we experience the bond of being truly known and unconditionally accepted.

My friend Brittany is right in the middle of trying to find that kind of relationship in her hometown. Three years ago, she moved about one hundred miles to a new town. Fortunately, she has one such close relationship in her old town, so she makes it a point to drive the two hours to visit that friend monthly. But a hundred miles is too far away to arrange for a quick coffee break to share a rough day or to grab a meal together and bask in the laughter and tears and comfort of her dear friend. Of course, she and her dear friend still text and email and call, but Brittany has more and more often in this past year become aware of the fact that she's lonely in her new town.

She has been hoping she might find another such friend at church. It took Brittany about a year to find a new church home. She is two years into belonging there and still keeping her eyes open. It has taken this long for her just to build up a group of acquaintances to chat comfortably with on

Sunday mornings—women with whom she at least shares a warm greeting that goes beyond the shallow, "Good to see you. How was your week?" kind of chat.

"This is slow going," Brittany told me. "I had hoped by now I would have found at least one woman with whom I felt the stirrings of a deeper bond. I know that part of my problem is that I'm not plugged into a ministry where I'm serving side by side with other people. Often it takes that kind of experience to break into more meaningful connections that might lead to something deeper. My best hope right now is a few of the women in the small group I've been a part of for about a year. We meet weekly for Bible study and are slowly getting to know one another's stories. It's a start."

Yes, a start. Of a process that takes time. And time can move slowly when you're lonely, can't it?

"But I'm so fortunate," Brittany says. "I have several deep, rich friendships in my life, even if they are far away. There's my friend in my old hometown who I see monthly. There's another precious friend in North Carolina who, though I rarely see face-to-face even yearly, I usually am in touch with a few times a week by text and email and phone. Beyond that, I have an intimate connection with Jesus who satisfies my deepest longings."

Can Jesus Satisfy Your Loneliness?

What do you honestly think? Is it possible to have the kind of friendship with Jesus, and with our heavenly Father, that truly satisfies our deepest longings to be fully known and unconditionally loved? For my part, I'm grateful to be able to say yes to that question. Like Brittany, I have found that such a relationship with God doesn't *replace* the longing for a human friend but provides me with a firm foundation of knowing I am loved unconditionally and nourishes my need for intimacy. I'm a single woman. It is Jesus above all others who satisfies my deepest longing for intimacy. But in all honesty, I need to work at that to keep it real.

I'd love to say that many believers feel a deeply satisfying intimacy with Jesus that meets their core need to be known. But from my years in ministry and my years of friendships, I know otherwise. For far too many of us, that spiritual relationship is either too removed from earthly life or too weighed down with emotional baggage to literally satisfy our deepest longings.

This is one reason I spent two chapters discussing solitude. It takes *time with Him*, just as in our earthly relationships, to create that bond with Jesus. And it takes *time in the Word* as well.

You probably know that David is called "a man after God's own heart." I suggest that we invest time in some of his Psalms—written in his times of solitude with God—to seek enriching our friendship with God. Let's turn to Psalm 139; there we find David speaking about his own longing to be known.

As you read, make this Scripture your prayer. Speak to God and ask Him to make these words real in your life. The first verse is worth memorizing and frequently repeating.

> O LORD, You have searched me and known me. (Ps. 139:1)

Do you see what I mean? David, too, longed to be known and was intimately aware that God knew everything about him. The same is true for you.

> You know when I sit down and when I rise up;
> You understand my thought from afar.
> You scrutinize my path and my lying down,
> And are intimately acquainted with all my ways.
> Even before there is a word on my tongue,
> Behold, O LORD, You know it all. (vv. 2–4)

There is no one on earth who knows you better than God. No one. Take your time right now. Reread those words. Meditate on them. Ask God to make them real to you.

> For You formed my inward parts;
> You wove me in my mother's womb.
> I will give thanks to You, for I am fearfully and
>   wonderfully made;
> Wonderful are Your works,
> And my soul knows it very well. (vv. 13–14)

Does your soul know it "very well"? I don't know about you, but my soul needs to know it a whole lot better! *Dear Lord, help me to know Your works—and Your deep intimate love for me—far better than I already do. Amen.*

> My frame was not hidden from You
> When I was made in secret,
> And skillfully wrought in the depths of the earth;
> Your eyes have seen my unformed substance. (vv.
>   15–16)

What is your "unformed substance"? It is your spirit. Your essence. The very core of who you are. God sees you—knows you—better than you know yourself.

> Search me, O God, and know my heart;
> Try me and know my anxious thoughts;
> And see if there be any hurtful way in me,
> And lead me in the everlasting way. (vv. 23–24)

Whatever you are worried or troubled about, whatever inside you is hurtful or ugly, or you are ashamed of or wish you could fix, God knows it inside and out. Ask Him, now, to lead you into the most intimate relationship with Him possible. You are going to spend all eternity with Him. You can begin *now* to richly enjoy His presence. With Jesus you truly can be fully known and never alone.

I can relate to what Brittany said about the time it takes to find and explore and build an intimate friendship: "This is slow going." Yes, it is. Transforming your relationship with God from where it is now to where it could be is slow going. But we each have to start somewhere! Start by reading and praying the words of Psalm 139 this week, asking God to make it real to you.

From Outsider to Insider

In elementary school, little groups of friends form. They have their own special secrets and ways. Maybe you were part of one of those groups. Maybe you weren't. If you were, then you felt more confident and shared in all the group did. You shared the same interests, played the same sports, were in the same classes, wore the same brands. You felt included. You were in the "in" crowd.

Well, I will confess to you that I have never been "in." I've always felt a little left out. It's not a good feeling. I've seen a friend's refrigerator dotted with invitations I did not receive and found out friends gathered and I was not included. I have described this as "always on the outside looking in."

John, the very close friend of Jesus, must have had a tender heart, for he tells a story of intense intimacy in John 20. It is the story of Thomas. I invite you to see it with fresh eyes, thinking about your own friendship with Jesus and the closeness you'd like to experience with Him.

"On the outside looking in" was probably an unusual feeling for the disciple Thomas. He was a twin, so he'd probably always had someone with whom he felt a strong bond. Thomas said he was willing to die with Jesus. He was the one who asked Jesus, "Lord, we do not know where You are going, how do we know the way?" And Jesus gave that great statement in response: "I am the way, and the truth, and the life; no one comes to the Father but through Me" (John 14:5–6). But now Thomas was in the room with the other disciples as they were excitedly talking about having seen the risen Jesus.

It was hard to take in. Was it really true? Could it be true? He had his doubts. He hadn't been with the other disciples when they found the empty tomb or when Jesus had physically revealed Himself to them after the resurrection. Now he was hearing it all secondhand, and it was just too much to believe. Too good to believe. He wanted to believe his friends but could not. He told the others, "Unless I see in His hands the imprint of the nails, and put my finger into the place of the nails, and put my hand into His side, I will not believe" (John 20:25). He wanted proof!

That must have put him on the outs with the other disciples. I can just hear them arguing with him. "But, Thomas, it really was Him. Don't you believe us?" And Thomas would reply, "Not until I see with my own eyes." Round and round it went—for eight days! Thomas wanted substantial evidence. He was alone in his thinking and doubts—the others believed and were excited. He was also the odd man out in not having experienced the incredible meeting with Jesus. That, too, must have felt isolating. *How come everyone else got to see Jesus and he didn't?* he must have wondered. Did the other disciples begin to treat him differently? Make him feel like he was not a part of them anymore?

They gathered together again, and this time Thomas was with them. The doors were closed and probably locked. Were they still afraid of the Roman guards? All of a sudden there was Jesus, standing in the middle of them. He hadn't knocked or opened the door—He just appeared!

I would love to know the expression on Thomas's face. Awe? Fear? Relief? Tears?

Jesus said to them all, "Peace be with you" (v. 26).

Then He turned His laser-like attention to Thomas. Boy! I bet you could have heard a pin drop. I am sure they were all wondering what Jesus was going to say to Thomas. Was He going to scold Thomas for his doubts? Was He going to give Thomas a discourse on unbelief? Was He going to push Thomas further out of the circle?

Jesus did none of those things. In fact, He asked Thomas to come closer. Jesus then invited Thomas to reach with his fingers into the scars on His hands. Can you imagine Thomas's feelings at that moment? Jesus knew exactly what he had told the other disciples. Of all the things the risen Lord might have had on His mind, He was focused on Thomas and his doubts. Did Thomas reach hesitantly? Did he touch oh so gently? Then Jesus spoke to him again. I imagine His eyes were locked on Thomas's and that Thomas's eyes were full of tears. "Reach here your hand and put it into My side," He said (v. 27).

Jesus must have opened His robe to reveal His wound. Such a tender moment.

Jesus's invitation is always, "Come." *Come to Me with your doubts. Come to Me if you feel left out or marginalized. Come to Me if you feel distant and alone.* Jesus welcomes you with open arms and gives you access—up close and personal. An invitation to know Him better, more intimately.

There was no condemnation for Thomas's doubt. He was an honest doubter. He didn't doubt to keep Jesus out but rather asked his questions because he wanted to know Jesus more fully. And Jesus gave him full access to His person. Jesus told him, "Do not be unbelieving, but believing" (v. 27).

Thomas was overwhelmed and said, "My Lord and my God!" (v. 28). All his doubts vanished. He knew he was in the presence of Jesus.

In the presence of Jesus may all of your doubts and all of mine vanish as well. May our sense of distance from Him vanish. May we more fully know intimacy with Him.

Tradition tells us that Thomas became a missionary to India. I love the thought of him spending the rest of his life telling of the risen Christ to those who didn't know Him.

Vulnerability with Jesus

Thomas was certainly vulnerable with his friends, wasn't he, when they were all trying so hard to convince him that Jesus had risen? In all likelihood he was under a lot of pressure to believe their eyewitness accounts of Jesus's appearance, but he would not compromise his honesty. He couldn't believe. And he confessed that to them openly. "Vulnerability is not weakness; it is our most accurate measure of courage," writes Brené Brown.[4] I respect that kind of courageous transparency, for it might have been tempting to simply go along with their story and act as if he did believe just to take the pressure off. He could have kept his doubts to himself like we often do. Am I right? Do you sometimes hide the doubts you have about God from those you trust? Would your relationships grow deeper if you were willing to confess your doubts? I suspect they would. Vulnerability and transparency are the building blocks of intimate friendship.

Of all the characters in the Gospels there is one man who stands out to me as having the boldest and most powerful faith, above all the others: John the Baptist. Until recently I would have never described John as vulnerable. Bold, yes. Self-assured. Immovable. Unshakable. Rock solid. Irrepressible. Those are the words that come to my mind when I think of John thundering out in the wilderness, calling the crowds to repentance. But when we take a close look, we find that John, too, understood the importance of being vulnerable with his friends and with Jesus.

In Luke 7 we find John in prison. He had publicly denounced Herod for taking his sister-in-law as his lover. Such integrity even in the face of danger! He didn't compromise. He had embarrassed Herod and his family, and Herod couldn't let John go unpunished. He had the prophet thrown into prison.

It's hard to imagine the larger-than-life presence of John the Baptist confined to a prison cell. John was a man of action, a man of the wilderness, now wasting away in Herod's putrid prison. Meanwhile, Jesus's ministry was growing and on the move in a huge way. The multitudes were flocking to Him as He taught and healed and worked miracles and changed lives. What must that have been like for John? His disciples visited him in prison and reported all of these things, but John himself, like Thomas above, was now on the outside looking in, hearing the reports secondhand. After all his time preparing a way in the wilderness he was missing out on the action. Did he feel claustrophobic? Left out? Frustrated? Did he have doubts about God? About his ministry? Was he wondering if he was being denied the thrill of seeing Jesus in action because he was being punished for some reason?

Scripture doesn't tell us what all was running through John's mind. But John was human like you and me. Perhaps John's disciples had told him all that was going on, but then said, "But the great teacher doesn't go any further than healing and teaching. Nothing is being said about God's kingdom being set up to deliver the people from the bondage of Rome. And when the crowds get all worked up and excited, this great teacher withdraws by himself. Do you think he's the Messiah we've all been waiting for and talking about? He's not acting like it."

Did they plant doubt and fear in John? People can do that to us, if we let them. Or had doubts been growing in his mind in the endless hours of lonely confinement? What we do know for sure is that John summoned two of his disciples and entrusted them with a deeply personal and vulnerable question. Perhaps this question is the most poignant verse in Scripture, for it shows John's humanness. I am glad it was included. If the Gospels hadn't shown John had doubts, we'd never have gotten this glimpse into his heart. The verse reads, "[John] sent them to the Lord to ask him, 'Are you the Messiah we've been expecting, or should we keep looking for someone else?'" (Luke 7:19 NLT).

This couldn't have been easy to ask! John was Jesus's cousin. He must have heard his own mother, Elizabeth, tell the story of him leaping in her womb when she saw Mary pregnant with Jesus. It was John who'd baptized Jesus. He'd been there when the heavens opened and the Holy Spirit descended upon Jesus in bodily form like a dove, and a voice came from heaven, "This is My beloved Son, in whom I am well-pleased" (Matt. 3:17).

It was John who declared to the people who'd come to hear him preach, saying of Jesus, "Behold, the Lamb of God who takes away the sin of the world!" (John 1:29).

Had captivity put a tremor in his heart?

John was asking, "Are you the One, or have I made a mistake? I've traveled everywhere talking about the coming kingdom of God. Should I look elsewhere?" He was unsure.

He had questions. And he made himself vulnerable enough to ask them.

What about you? Do you have doubts? Are you frustrated by what feels like a great distance between you and Jesus? You, too, can be vulnerable enough with Jesus to ask if He is real. If He will make Himself known to you, personally. Intimately.

Oh, how I would love to see exactly what happened when John's two disciples went to see Jesus. When they arrived, He was busy in the midst of a crowd. But that was okay. Jesus never minded interruptions. He probably knew and recognized the two as they approached Him. He loved them. Jesus listened as they asked John's question, though we know

He already knew what was coming. He always hears our questions before we ask.

Jesus knew John's heartbeat. And Jesus answered as only He can.

He replies to our questions not with harshness but with gentleness, in a way that answers so many doubts. His divinity meets our humanness as He points us to the larger picture, God's eternal purpose, always leading us to the next step.

Jesus's answer to John pointed to the facts and let John's disciples see for themselves:

> The blind can see.
> The lame can walk.
> The lepers are made clean.
> The deaf hear.
> The dead are raised up.
> And the poor have the Gospel preached to them.
> Go tell John these things. (Luke 7:22, my
> paraphrase)

His words no doubt remind John of Isaiah's prophecy in Isaiah 61:1,

> The Spirit of the Lord GOD is upon me,
> Because the LORD anointed me
> To bring good news to the afflicted;
> He has sent me to bind up the brokenhearted,
> To proclaim liberty to captives
> And freedom to prisoners.

Are you lonely? Doubting? Isolated? John was. So he was vulnerable with Jesus, and Jesus pointed John to the things that would not only identify Him as the Messiah but also encourage John's faith. Ask Him to do the same for you.

REACH

Now is the opportunity for you, too, to reach out and touch your risen Savior through the REACH exercise. The more you do so, the more certain you will become that you are fully known and never alone.

R—Recognize your longing to feel known by God and by a friend.

E—Express to God, *Lord, I need to feel known. By You and by others—by some close friend.*

A—Anticipate God will transform your loneliness for Him and for friendship into something positive. *Lord, I anticipate that You will fill me with assurance of Your intimate knowledge of me and the same kind of nonjudgmental love and tenderness for me as You showed to Thomas. And I thank You ahead of time.*

C—Connect with God by making some time in the next day to spend in solitude reading Psalm 139 and meditating on it. Connect with someone else by choosing a person over the next week to speak to. It could be as simple as a chat, like Alison on her chat bench. Just be intentional about showing interest in someone's life. Ask a few questions about their family or their story and listen well. I often like to start a conversation with, "Have you always lived in this area?"

Remember, your loneliness to be known can be transformed into your choice to know others.

H—Honor God by making your need to feel known sacred. In other words, dedicate that need to God and His use. This prayer may help: *Lord, I offer to You my need to be known. Thank You for knowing me fully and still loving and accepting me. Help me to reach out to others in such a way that I invite mutual transparency and vulnerability so that we both will be known. Amen.*

O Lord, You have searched me and known me.

Psalm 139:1

12

The Security of Belonging

Our friendship with Jesus is personal but not private. To be connected to Jesus in friendship is to be connected to his friends as well.

Trevor Hudson[1]

The deep rumbling sound of the engine was so invasive it seemed to be rattling my bones. Is that why I was trembling? Or was it actually my nervousness—or excitement? Probably all three. I looked over at Todd, my son-in-law. He was watching me, mischievously grinning ear to ear, anticipation written all over his face. I tried to shift my weight to get more comfortable, but could barely move without bumping into the man sitting next to me on the floor of the plane. We were packed like sardines on our way to thirteen thousand feet. I had to laugh. Was I really about to jump out of an airplane?

Just the previous week I'd been rafting down the Pigeon River in East Tennessee with my family—my son, Graham, my two daughters, Noelle and Windsor, their husbands, Maury and Todd, and my two older grandsons, Walker and

Zach. It was a great family experience filled with laughter and no small amount of getting drenched. As we loaded into the cars to go home I casually mentioned I'd always wanted to skydive; it was on my "bucket list." Todd heard me and said he'd like to as well. Clearly, he was very serious. He called the skydiving company near my home and made reservations for the following Saturday. (There was no backing out now!)

On Saturday morning, all of us got up early and drove to the airport—my family wanted to see me do this. They thought I was crazy. I began to think I was too! But Todd's excitement emboldened me. He and I suited up and were instructed on how to do a tandem dive. There were others doing the same thing. Our group had about eight or ten people, each with their own tandem instructor. Before I knew it, we were in the plane to take us up.

We were buckled in tightly with our instructors—as tightly as two can be without being married. I tried to swallow but my mouth had gone dry.

The first team jumped. *I guess I'm really going to go through with this,* I thought as my buddy and I scooted forward, closer to the door. I was near the back and it was surreal to watch my classmates in front of me disappear out the wide cargo door. Then I watched as Todd disappeared.

Before I knew it, I was seated on the edge with my tandem jumper. The roaring of the wind and the droning of the engine deafened me so that I could barely hear the instructor as he shouted, "Go, go." And just like that, I leaned forward and was out! I was free-falling at a speed of about two hundred miles per hour, a very uncomfortable feeling—but an immediate facelift! The instructor told me to stand on his feet because he needed to loosen my harness. *You have to be kidding!* I thought. But I did as I was told. When he loosened my harness I was more comfortable, and he then opened the parachute. We slowed down and I could enjoy the view. The closer we got to earth, the stronger the queasy feeling I get on roller coasters became. But soon we landed—on our feet, as instructed!

Todd had landed before me and he greeted me with a big smile, as did the rest of the family. As we tell the story now, he says he always wanted to be able to say he pushed his mother-in-law out of a plane!

Would I jump again? No. But it does make for fun conversations, and that day has taken its place among the many family stories we love to retell.

We each seem to play our roles in the family. Todd definitely holds the title as our adventurer. He's married to my younger daughter, Windsor, who's our whiz at math. She has her real estate and insurance licenses. Her sister, Noelle, is a nurse. She always advises us to work on healthy practices like exercise and our eating habits—met with rolled eyes but thankfulness. Her husband, Maury, is our computer expert, and when I have technical difficulties he is always available to get it set right. He is very steady and calm. Graham, the middle child, knows all things about automobiles and houses. Anytime we need a car, we call him for advice. He is also our funny man. He makes us laugh—mainly at ourselves. Each member of the family brings something to the table. Each is valuable. Each is loved. Each is vitally important to the whole.

I come from a very large family. My father had four siblings, as did my mother, and there are a lot of cousins on both sides. While we do not see each other often, we always enjoy each other. I have two older sisters and two younger brothers. We all have children, and they all have children. At my father's funeral, we had over two hundred family members present!

Family has been the single most important influence in my life, as it is for most people. Family is where a child learns to relate to the world. It is the context where, in a healthy family, parents nurture and provide safety as well as guidance until children are of age to navigate on their own. A family meets the basic needs of its children—and often of its older members, the elderly. And hopefully, a family is a built-in support system providing unconditional love. A family gives us a sense of belonging, and that is one of our basic needs as human beings according to Maslow's hierarchy of needs.

Belonging. Even the sound of that word is warm and comforting.

Belonging to God

God is "head of household" in the family of God. What does that mean, especially to those of us who feel lonely? It means we have a place in a family where we belong, with God as our Father. The Bible says,

> For all who are being led by the Spirit of God, these are sons of God. For you have not received a spirit of slavery leading to fear again, but you have received a spirit of adoption as sons by which we cry out, "Abba! Father!" (Rom. 8:14–15)

What an amazing thought! We are adopted into the very family of God, and that's better than being adopted by any royal family!

202

That word *Abba* means "Papa" or "Daddy." It is a term of familiarity, affection, and love. We can run into the very throne room of heaven and reach up for our Father. He will reach down, pull us into His arms, and draw us close. Pause a moment and imagine that. As a Father, God loves to give good things to His children. One of the good things He has given us, as believers, is the Holy Spirit. "The Spirit Himself testifies with our spirit that we are children of God, and if children, heirs also, heirs of God and fellow heirs with Christ" (vv. 16–17).

In spite of this truth, many lonely believers feel that God seems far away. Distant. Do you? What would make you feel more connected to Him? How can your relationship with God be transformed into a greater sense of belonging?

I suggest that far too many of us think that as long as we are connected to God as our Abba Father, that should be enough. Then we scratch our heads when we still feel lonely. The truth is, if we stop there, we are missing an absolutely essential piece of being part of the family of God. Can you guess what it is? It's spending time with the rest of the family!

Lynn learned this the hard way, but realizing it has changed not only her own life but the lives of many others.

Lonely but Courageous

Lynn is a kind, caring, and quiet woman. She has always been an introvert. During her childhood years she appreciated the friendships of a very small group of friends, but it wasn't her nature to reach out and connect with a wider circle of other kids. Even in school, though she invariably knew the answers to questions the teachers asked, she rarely raised her hand. She seemed content to stay in the background rather than draw attention to herself. When she did make friends, they invariably discovered her to be witty, highly intelligent, and extremely loyal. One-on-one she did fine, but in groups of people she often felt she was on the outside looking in.

While in college Lynn had a small group of close friends whom she trusted implicitly. Then, tragically, a few of those friends betrayed her trust and wounded her deeply. Perhaps, had she reached out to others for healing and support, she would have recovered more easily, but who was there to reach out to? Her closest friends were the ones who had wounded her. She kept her pain to herself, and that pain eroded any desire to seek out new connections. To make matters considerably worse, while she didn't know it at the time, she had a chemical imbalance that was leading her into depression. Over a period of about a year she slipped further and further into a deep clinical depression. She couldn't work. She grew isolated and descended into a very dark place. There she stayed for five long years. Her only real connections were with her parents and her sister. But they weren't enough. She was desperately lonely.

Eventually, she climbed out of that pit and reengaged with the world to some extent. But in many ways, she remained emotionally withdrawn and alone—with the exception, once again, of a very few special friendships.

Sadly, Lynn's depression returned with a vengeance. This time she was able to seek medical help and counseling, but the battle with her brain chemistry, she discovered over time, would be a battle she would need to fight for the rest of her life. Loneliness continued to be a significant part of her struggle.

When Lynn was in her forties, she began seeing one particular counselor who really seemed to "get" her. Though Lynn's purpose in their sessions was to equip her to deal with depression, the counselor helped Lynn see how very small her circle of relationships really was and challenged her to set about intentionally growing that circle.

"Human beings are social creatures," states an article in *News in Health.* "Feeling like we're part of a community helps us thrive. But we sometimes have a hard time making and keeping the relationships that sustain us."[2] That was true of Lynn. Tentatively she began to intentionally explore acquaintances to see if they might become friends. It took a lot of trial and error. It also took courage. Some people would reciprocate, others would not. She'd find herself getting her hopes up that a getting-to-know-you lunch might spark a genuine friendship, then being disappointed when it didn't. Other times she held out hope in a new relationship only to encounter judgment or a lack of authenticity—both of which Lynn found deadly in a genuine friendship.

But she kept at it. She became especially adept at reaching out to lonely women—those more on the fringes of the social circles at church or work. It was never easy for her to put herself out there for that initial contact or invitation, especially if she was feeling depressed, but she was determined, so in spite of the awkward discomfort she felt, she truly was courageous and kept on trying. One day it occurred to her to plan an outing to a cute little nearby town for some antique shopping. In a bold step, she invited a handful of women this time, some of whom didn't know one another. Five women accepted! The trip was a huge success, with the women asking Lynn, "What are you planning next?" Because Lynn was acting as host of the group, she felt like she belonged rather than like an outsider.

Pam Rhodes, in her foreword to the book *Freedom from Loneliness*, wrote,

> The outside world can seem fearful and frightening—but the sense that you are all alone can bring a different sort of fear, that perhaps no one will ever break through your lonely shell—or, worse still, that no one will ever want to. Loneliness makes you question your worth, your appearance, your character, your whole being. . . . It saps your confidence.[3]

Lynn knew what it felt like to fear that no one would ever break through her shell. For years her confidence had been sapped. But now it was beginning to grow.

Delighted at the bond that was forming among several of the women, Lynn planned another trip about six weeks later—this time to a huge craft festival about an hour away. She cast her net a bit wider, and if someone declined she looked for another woman to take her place. Trip two got rave reviews, and Lynn discovered she now had a reputation for planning fun outings. She also watched with great satisfaction as some of the women who'd met each other on her trip became friends with one another.

As Lynn continued in her newfound role as a "connector" of women, her social confidence grew. She moved from being reticent to "put herself out there" to looking forward to saying hi to new folks and lonely people at church.

This was two decades ago. Lynn still wages her battle with depression as a single woman in her sixties and every few years has to work diligently with her doctors to find the new balance of medications that will restore her lest she slide back down into darkness. But she is no longer plagued by loneliness. And when she does feel lonely, she takes action. Today, Lynn has a very healthy circle of meaningful friendships, some that are brand-new and some that span up to twenty years. She is known in her church for connecting people to one another and having a real knack for creating a mix of people with a variety of interests and backgrounds who are likely to relate well with one another regardless of their differences. She also keeps an eye out for newcomers and people sitting alone and greets them warmly. What's more, she is very aware of how important her social connections are to keeping her depression at bay. They are part of her self-care. She attests to the truth of this quote:

> When we feel connected, we are generally less agitated and less stressed than when we feel lonely. In general, feeling connected also lowers feelings of hostility and depression. All of which can have profoundly positive influences on our health.[4]

Lynn just planned another outing last month where new friendships were forged, laughter and meaningful conversation filled the day, and once again the day ended with a few of the women saying, "That was great fun. Thanks so much for inviting me. What are you planning next?"

Friendship with God's People Is Essential to Our Souls

Lynn had no magic formula for moving from "friendship poor" to "friendship rich." It really came down to first understanding her design, which gave her a sense of purpose. Then she chose to be intentional about building new friendships and also chose her role as one who offered invitations rather than waited for them. She dove deep with those friends who clicked and took on the purpose of helping others connect. It all required courage and dedication.

So, to address meeting your need to belong, we're going to talk about design, purpose, role, and intentionality.

As mentioned earlier, Jesus's prayer in John 17 is often called His High Priestly Prayer, because for much of it He was praying for His disciples. And not for them only "but for those also who believe in Me through their word" (v. 20). That would be you and me! He fervently prayed, "Holy Father, keep them in Your name, the name which You have given Me, that they may be one even as We are" (v. 11).

He wants us to be deeply connected to one another, so much so that we are "one." We were built for community with one another. It's in our DNA. That is why loneliness can be so painful.

When we are in community with others in the body of Christ, we are in fellowship with other human beings who experience the spiritual aspect of life as we do—with all its joys and trials. An Angus Reid Institute poll of Canadians found that religion can play a key role in reducing social isolation and loneliness and that faith communities are fairly successful at bringing people together and reaching those who are isolated.[5] Of course, we may not all see things the same way or feel the same way about them—and I think that is the beauty of fellowship. The Scripture says, "Iron sharpens iron, so one man sharpens another" (Prov. 27:17). Community is not always easy, and it can be messy. But it is what God has given us. "Fellowship is a mutual bond that Christians have with Christ that puts us in a deep, eternal relationship with one another," says John Piper.[6] Paul describes this in 1 Corinthians 12 when he writes about the body having many members but still being one body. That is who we are as believers. We are part of Christ's body, and that is our community.

In this body of Christ, we have each been given gifts to use for the benefit of the whole. The apostle Paul lists some of these gifts and their use in 1 Corinthians 12–14. He writes,

> Now there are varieties of gifts, but the same Spirit. And there are varieties of ministries, and the same Lord. There are varieties of effects, but the same God who works all things in all persons. But to each one is given the manifestation of the Spirit for the common good. (12:4–7)

Paul goes on to mention some of the gifts, like the word of wisdom, the word of knowledge, faith, healing, and so on. He lists apostles, prophets, teachers, and others, "for the equipping of the saints for the work of service, to the building up of the body of Christ" (Eph. 4:12). If you want to see a longer list, look up these Scriptures and others in the Bible. There is not one single, exhaustive list, but I think it's most important to notice the gifts are given for service—to build up the body of Christ, the family of God, not to hoard or use selfishly. We are to use our gifts in the service of others, for all of them have been given to equip and edify the family of God. If you don't know what your gifting is, there are gift-finding tests you can take to get an idea of what they might be. I highly recommend *What You Do Best in the Body of Christ: Discover Your Spiritual Gifts, Personal Style, and God-Given Passion* by Bruce Bugbee. It is an excellent resource. You might even ask someone what they see as your gift—you might be surprised. Whatever your process, remember that the point to understand is that it is God's design to use each of us to strengthen and build up one another.

"Yes," you might be saying, "but if I'm lonely, how is that supposed to work?"

Remember Lynn? Design, purpose, role, and intentionality. Through Lynn's story we see that we are *designed*, even gifted, to connect with one another. We each have a *purpose* to build up and equip one another. We need others and others need us to accomplish that purpose. You, like Lynn, may need to explore precisely what *role* you want to serve. This may depend on your unique spiritual gifts. I suspect Lynn has the gift of hospitality. It is when she stepped into the role of hosting events that she blossomed, and she's gifted at making people feel part of a group. That leaves *intentionality*.

Consider that you, like Lynn, may need to become the one who reaches out to others rather than waiting and hoping that others will reach out to you. I know this may not be easy. It may take courage. It may result in some pain and disappointment along the way—but there is only one way through it, and that is to do it.

I can almost hear your frustration at this point. When you are hurting in loneliness you often don't feel like you have the energy or the wherewithal to step out. But remember, sometimes the pain of loneliness is what becomes our motivation for change. Lynn worked at it and changed her behavior. You can too. You are gifted to be a gift!

Elle wrote to me about her loneliness. Her experience illustrates this very point.

I was new to my job at a large ministry—and new to the city, three states away from my own. My teenage daughter, not happy with the change in school or location, had moved with me. Yet within weeks she was off and socializing with new friends while I was left alone. The people at my job were wonderful. Friendly, fun, kind. But they were also very busy with their own families and friends they had already. I spent many months feeling quite happy at work and ever so lonely at home. Weekends were the absolute worst. After a year, I knew if I wanted to develop friendships at all, I was going to have to figure out a different way to approach the dilemma.

So, I decided to invite every woman of my age range to a ladies' monthly lunch out. It didn't take long for friendships to begin to grow outside work. One woman complained her husband wouldn't watch chick flicks, so we began to have a casual dessert potluck and chick flick nights at my house. Eventually, four of us became the best of friends and met frequently at each other's houses for laughter and chats and discussions about the difficult things in our lives. Oh, what I would have missed if I hadn't forced myself to get beyond my fear and what seemed to be a brick wall keeping me from friendships.

Elle stepped up and stepped out. Those of us who long to feel that we belong have to do the same thing. Remember, as we share our gifts, others will benefit as well as share their own with us. The whole body grows stronger.

Practical Advice

I turned to the military spouses for some practical insights here, as one challenge they face is that they frequently have to relocate. This makes them well-experienced at living with and working to overcome loneliness. I asked for tips or advice, and they didn't disappoint. Corie said, "We have moved so much we don't have a church home; [we] have to start over every time, and it takes at least six months to find and benefit from a growing friendship."

It must be hard repeating that pattern time and time again. A number of them said they longed for a sense of community. Several said they felt unneeded where they are. Jackie explained that she needed "companionship, friendship, empathy, compassion, and affirmation." Do you know that feeling?

Corie also said she longed for "a consistent friend, and a familiar church where I can worship freely and feel the warm greetings of familiar faces." We can all relate to that, can't we?

Liz longed for a hug. Oh, I can empathize with that. I often long for a hug myself. I remember that in my postdivorce days I literally ached to be hugged. (I'll talk more about that in the next chapter.)

So, what advice do these spouses have for lonely people? Meg wrote, "Being committed to a local body of believers is an integral part of fighting the battle against loneliness." Cynthia made a fascinating comment: "Be the community you wish you had, and you'll eventually find yourself surrounded by people." That's exactly what Lynn and Elle did.

Cynthia also wrote, "Vulnerability breeds vulnerability." We discussed that in chapter 11. Vulnerability is crucial to deep friendships, but often others won't risk it until we ourselves become vulnerable to them. Modeling vulnerability also dovetails with her comment above that we need to be the community we wish we had.

Cynthia also explained that what helped her the most in coping with loneliness was to be included in a small group of women who pray for one another and who would invite her out or to come over and "do life with me." But it sounds like Cynthia understands that you may need to be the initiator.

Kori's message was similar. "I find lots of folks are looking for community, [but] not very many of them start building it on their own. They wait to be invited, instead of inviting." That can be a very long wait. The invitation may never come! Beth agreed. Her advice was, "Become more outgoing and be willing to take the first step in forming new friendships by inviting others to do activities with you and by being vulnerable."

Kori used the word *intentionally* two times when she explained that what helped her was "being intentional about building community" (finding a church home, inviting people into her home, etc.) and finding those "friends for life" and intentionally staying in touch with them.

Are you catching on to a theme here? These women have faced moves and deployments time and time again, and all their advice points to the reality that it is the lonely person who must often take the first step.

I realize this may not be what you want to hear. Change is seldom easy. But being lonely isn't easy either, and it's dangerous to your health and your spiritual well-being.

For myself, I had to start with small steps. But it really helped to understand that we were created for community, to be part of a family—the family of God. Find a body of believers to worship with, then ask for your Father's help in using your gifts to create a community for others and thereby enrich your relationships. One idea is to consider asking your pastor where you can best serve in the church—they love to hear that.

Author Annie Lent writes, "Inviting God's love to fill your loneliness takes some soul care. His love builds the secure foundation from which you can take the risky and scary steps of inviting people into your life."[7]

Yes, some soul care is needed for us to internalize the security of belonging, but with that care we will be able to take some risky yet necessary steps. The rewards will be rich. The greater our intimacy with God, the bolder we can be in our intimacy with the body of Christ, and the greater our intimacy with the body of Christ, the greater our intimacy with God. God designed it that way on purpose.

I've focused our attention in this chapter primarily on belonging to the community of the family of God. However, there are many other communities to be a part of—your neighborhood, your town, your state, and groups of people who share your interests. Yes, sometimes we have to force ourselves to "get out there." When we are in the dark places of loneliness, that can seem very hard to do, but it is worth the effort. If you don't have a community you feel you belong to, begin to volunteer. Or start your own group. Remember, joining a group is not only a good remedy for loneliness but is good for your health. Researchers at the University of Queensland in Australia, for example, have found that older adults who take part in social groups such as book clubs or church groups have a lower risk of death.[8]

Dr. Francie Hart Broghammer, in her essay "Death by Loneliness," gives us some wonderfully practical advice:

> There is no straightforward solution to our current problem, but everyone can play a role in helping America heal. The first step: be present. Close your computer and engage your colleague while waiting for a meeting to start. Re-define "FaceTime" by opting for a shared coffee instead of a phone call. Check in on the widow down the street. Recognize the sacred space of the home, by designating "tech-free" spaces. Reclaim the dinner table and engage in religious and other institutions of civic life. In short, re-cultivate the virtues of association and community.[9]

We were created for community, to be part of a family where we are well-connected and mutually meet one another's needs. As such we are to play our part by using our gifts, and as others do the same, we are both giving and receiving as God intended. As we know and experience this, we can use our gifts to create a community for others and thereby enrich our relationships and enrich the family of God. When we do so, our loneliness and longing to feel we belong have been transformed into letting others know that they belong.

REACH

Today, let's switch it up a little bit and turn the entire REACH exercise into a prayer.

R—Lord, I *recognize* that my need to belong is first meant to be met in You, and then in my relationships with others in the body of Christ.

E—Lord, I *express* to You that while I may feel hesitant to change, I realize I need to change if I want different results.

A—Lord, I *anticipate* that You will inspire me to invest more time and energy in growing my intimacy with You and that You will lessen my hesitancy about risking reaching out to someone else.

C—*Connect* me, Lord, in a fresh way to Your Word so that it may come alive to me and help me experience the sense of belonging You want me to have. And *connect* me to at least one new person with whom I might take a first step in testing the waters of friendship.

H—Lord, I want to *honor* You by making my loneliness sacred. I understand that means I need to dedicate it to You and Your purposes, and so I do. Use me, Lord, to meet someone else's need. Amen.

Bear one another's burdens, and thereby fulfill the law of Christ.

Galatians 6:2

13

The Assurance of Being Loved

Let Him free us from ourselves in order that we may become the servants of others.

Elisabeth Elliot[1]

I tried not to stare at the man. I didn't want to be rude. But I had trouble looking away, as I was trying to understand what I was seeing. Part of the man's nose was missing and his hands were terribly disfigured—one of his thumbs was gone and several of his fingers were stumps. I felt afraid, though my grandfather had assured me I'd be safe.

I was eleven, traveling in South Korea with my grandfather Dr. L. Nelson Bell (my mother's father), who was on the Southern Presbyterian Church's World Mission Board. We were on a tour of several mission stations that included a leper colony. On the way to the colony, my grandfather had tried to prepare me by explaining some of what I'd be seeing, but I really hadn't understood until I saw it for myself. Over the next few hours, I was sad to see those with half their faces gone, hands that looked like claws, large growths on hands and arms, missing feet, and twisted bodies. My memory of the day is still vivid all these many years later.

Out of anxiety I began to chew my fingernails, and my grandfather and his companion gave me a stern admonition to stop. It was hard for me to understand how these people must feel watching their bodies become deformed. But I did understand that they were being well taken care of by the missionaries. They were receiving medical help and were given a place to live because they had to be kept away from society and family. My grandfather told me they were also hearing the gospel of Jesus. Still, how lonely it must have been to have to move away from their families and villages.

I knew Bible stories about lepers and wondered how they felt when they heard that Jesus had healed some lepers. Did they wonder if Jesus would heal them too? Or did they have no hope?

The Power of a Touch

Today we know leprosy, now called Hansen's disease, can be treated. But in Jesus's day, leprosy was dreaded and carried a painful stigma. Lepers were treated as if they were already dead—given, in essence, a living death sentence. As soon as his or her condition was diagnosed, the leper was immediately banished from human society. No exceptions. Whenever they went out in public, they couldn't get closer than eighteen inches to another person and had to shout out, "Unclean!" so people could jump out of the way and keep at a distance. People hid from them. They threw rocks at them. It was illegal for anyone to greet a leper.

Leviticus 13 spells out how lepers of that day were to be treated. If you had swelling, a scab, or a bright spot on your skin, you had to present yourself to a priest. Through a rather long process of examination and isolation, the priest would determine if it was leprosy. If it was, you were pronounced unclean and isolated from others until the priest declared you to be healed. Once declared clean by the priest, you were to bring two birds for sacrifice.

Of course, Jesus knew about leprosy and the suffering lepers endured physically, mentally, emotionally, and socially. He'd seen countless lepers. He could hear them call out "Unclean, unclean!" as they walked by.

One day Jesus was teaching, the crowd hanging on His words. They had never heard one teach with such authority. But He had a gentle, winsome way about Him. He made things understandable with stories they could relate to. The crowd grew.

And then a leper came. A man who longed for human touch. A man alone in his unbearable state. He was hungry for someone to care for him and therefore took a huge risk. He stepped into the crowd to get to Jesus. The crowd parted. No one wanted to be near him or even have their clothes touch where he walked. But they didn't disperse. They stayed to watch what would happen. Rabbis were known to run and hide from lepers rather than seek to alleviate their suffering. But Jesus did not run or shrink back. The leper went straight to Jesus and bowed down in front of him.

"Lord, if You are willing, You can make me clean," he said (Luke 5:12).

The leper called Him "Lord." (The King James Version says he "worshiped" Him.) What did he know of Jesus?

Had he listened from the fringes of the crowd to some of Jesus's teaching on the mountain? Perhaps he had heard of others being healed. Whatever he'd heard or seen had been enough that this man had come to see Jesus as "Lord" and addressed Him as such.

Jesus had compassion on him. He didn't turn away like other rabbis. The crowd watched with shock as Jesus reached out His hand and touched the leper. They couldn't believe their eyes. No one ever dared touch a leper.

"I am willing; be cleansed," the Lord said (v. 13). The use of the words "I am" would have sent an electric shock through the crowd. That was God's name. *Yahweh.* Jesus was claiming His authority over the disease, and we are told the leprosy was immediately cleansed.

I wonder how long it had been since anyone had touched this man. Jesus could have healed him with just a word, but He chose to touch him. What a gift. That touch spoke volumes. It spoke love.

I love the stories of Jesus touching people. When Peter's mother-in-law was ill with a fever, Jesus touched her hand and the fever left her. One time two blind men followed Jesus, begging for His mercy. He touched their eyes and they could see. When Jesus took Peter, James, and John up on a mountain to witness His transfiguration, a voice spoke from heaven and said, "'This is My beloved Son, with whom I am well-pleased; listen to Him!' When the disciples heard this, they fell face down to the ground and were terrified. And Jesus came to them and touched them and said, 'Get up, and do not be afraid'" (Matt. 17:5–7). Isn't that tender? I'm sure His touch reassured them and calmed their fear.

One day Jesus came across a funeral procession for a widow's son. He took compassion on the widow, stepped up and touched the coffin, and the man sat up! Once, a deaf man who also had trouble speaking was brought to Jesus. Jesus put His fingers in the man's ears, then spat and touched the man's tongue with His saliva, and the man was healed. Why did Jesus choose to touch in these instances, when it seems most times people were healed with just a word or simply by touching His garment? Jesus knew the hearts and stories and longings of each of these people. Surely, He knew that touch *mattered* to them.

So much love can be communicated with a touch.

I remember after divorce how I ached to be hugged or touched by someone. It meant the world to me when a friend would greet me with a hug. Touch can go so far in chasing away loneliness. It says, "I care. I love you." And we all ache to be loved.

Jesus's Most Important Instructions

We've talked in this book about the longing to be seen, to be chosen, to be known, and to belong. We've discussed how once we grasp that God meets those needs for us, we are able to reach out to others and meet those needs in them. When we do, we find that they often reach back to us, and so our needs are even better fulfilled. Well, I've saved the best for last—the longing *to be loved*. Is there a more powerful need inside the human heart than that? No. Above all else we were designed to be loved. God, whose love for us—for you individually—compelled Him to send Jesus to this earth to die that we might have eternal life with Him, knows that love is the most powerful force on earth as it is in heaven. "But now faith, hope, love abide these three; but the greatest of these is love" (1 Cor. 13:13). After all, God *is* love.

There is little wonder, then, that on the night when He knew He was about to be betrayed, He gave His final instructions to the disciples on this very topic. Jesus and His disciples had finished the Last Supper, and Jesus began to teach them. He had just finished His teaching about the vine and the branches. And then He said this:

> Just as the Father has loved Me, I have also loved you; abide in My love. If you keep My commandments, you will abide in My love; just as I have kept My Father's commandments and abide in His love. (John 15:9–10)

In the next verses He gave us His *reason* for telling us this, and it is such a wonderful reason.

> These things I have spoken to you so that My joy may be in you, and that your joy may be made full. This is My commandment, that you love one another, just as I have loved you. Greater love has no one than this, that one lay down his life for his friends. (vv. 11–13)

For those of us who are lonely, this is the most powerful thing He can tell us. He loves us so much He is willing to lay down His life for us. And He did so the very next day. Yes—no wonder He knew that would fill us with joy! He took our punishment. He felt the wrath of God for our sin willingly so we could live for all eternity with Him and the Father and the Spirit.

But there is another message in those words as well, and frankly, it makes one pause. It is a command that we love *just as He does*—that we, too, be willing to lay down our very lives for our "friends." Love, Jesus is saying, demands the ultimate sacrifice—not only *for* us, but *from* us. On the one hand, when I read those words, I know it's the right thing to do. It's a high calling to a higher purpose, but I see that and say, "Yes, Lord, I'm all in!"

On the other hand, however, I know it is easier said than done.

Sacrificial Love

The truth is, it's hard to sacrifice ourselves. It's hard enough to put others' needs above our own, let alone be willing to actually die for another. And to be honest, for those of us who are lonely, that might be doubly hard. Why? Because when we are lonely, we feel needy. We're seeking to have our needs met. And that doesn't exactly lend itself to self-sacrifice, does it?

And how, precisely, is sacrifice supposed to fill us with joy? If we are going to be honest, fear and self-protection seem far more likely a response than joy over the idea of sacrificing ourselves.

As usual, God's ways are not our ways, so I believe we are going to have to look beyond the obvious and the immediate to understand God's equation.

Debra Moerke's story sheds some light on this for me. See if you agree.

Debra and her husband, Al, had been foster parents over a seventeen-year period to over one hundred children when they were thrust into a heart-wrenching situation. They'd been fostering a four-year-old girl named Hannah and her four siblings when suddenly the court decided to return the five children to their mother, Karen. The Moerkes were alarmed. They'd been reporting to family services for several months some concerns about Karen possibly mistreating Hannah during her home visits. (The other children all seemed safe.) They pleaded with family services to delay Hannah's return until an investigation could be done to ensure Hannah's safety, but their pleading fell on deaf ears. They loved Hannah and even offered to adopt her. But the court decision was final. Debra tells a harrowing tale of little Hannah begging not to be taken back to her mother. She literally had to be pried, hysterical, from Debra's arms.

Months passed. Debra visited Karen and the children a number of times, but each time, little Hannah wasn't home. Karen always had an explanation—she was visiting friends, she had a birthday party to attend, and so on—but Debra was concerned. Each time she reported her concern and Hannah's absence to family services, she was assured they'd been doing home visits and that all was well.

Then one evening, Debra got a call from family services. Hannah's body had been found. Her mother had confessed to killing her and had been arrested. Debra writes, "I couldn't think. I could only feel pain everywhere, clawing at my stomach and ripping through my chest, squeezing breath and life out of me." She broke the news to Al and their other children. "We stood as a family, broken, devastated, our hearts and souls torn, grieving and mourning as we had never done before. Our legs gave way, and still embracing each other, we dropped to our knees on the carpet, drowning in our loss."[2]

The next morning Debra's phone rang again. It was the jail with a collect call from an inmate. Would she accept the charges? Debra could only think of one inmate—Karen. *Does she really think I would accept the charges and take her call? What is she thinking?* She was about to hang up but, "In that very second, a voice swept through my mind. 'If she were to call me, would I take her call?' My heart recognized the voice—Jesus. I froze. 'You are my hands and feet and voice. Do you represent me or not?'"[3]

Debra knew she had to take the call.

"Will you come see me?" Karen asked in a desperate whine. "I really need to see you."

At those words it seemed as if the world stopped spinning for a moment—time stood still. I tried to absorb her audacious request. Would I come see her? An unearthly rage surged up from some dark place inside of me. *See* her? I wanted to reach right through the phone and down her throat and rip her heart out of her body. . . . Then, just that quickly, the rage was gone, replaced by the echo of the words, "You are my hands and feet and voice. Do you represent me or not?"

[Debra told her,] "I don't know. I'll see."[4]

And Debra hung up. She detested the thought of visiting Karen, but in her heart, she already knew she'd go. Not because she wanted to. She would go simply out of obedience to Jesus.

"This is My commandment, that you love one another, just as I have loved you."

Easier said than done.

That evening Debra climbed into her car and drove to the jail. She felt so ill at the thought of facing Karen that at one point she had to pull off the road, afraid she was going to vomit. It took every ounce of determination she could muster to enter the jail and walk to the visitation cell. She felt rage. She felt sick. She wanted Karen to pay. She did not want to show love to the woman who had murdered little Hannah—the precious child whom she loved.

"These things I have spoken to you so that My joy may be in you, and that your joy may be made full. Greater love has no one than this, that a person will lay down his life for his friends."

How, I ask you, is loving Karen going to make Debra's joy full?

Debra's book, *Murder, Motherhood, and Miraculous Grace,* explores the depths of that question and more. The reality of sacrificial love is a hard road to walk. But just as Jesus carried His cross up the road to Golgotha, He beckons us to take up our crosses and follow Him. Angry or not. Hurting or not. Lonely or not. We are called to sacrificial love.

It's been about twenty years since Debra saw Karen in that visitation cell. When Karen walked in, Debra found herself embracing her. It defied all reason, but Jesus, in Debra, reached out and embraced the woman who murdered Debra's beloved Hannah. She touched her. And that touch spoke love to a murderer. Karen received life imprisonment without parole. But Debra, who has visited Karen faithfully for twenty years, has also had the privilege of leading Karen to faith in Jesus. Today the two are dear sisters in the Lord. Behind bars they laugh together, cry together, pray together, and share God's Word together.

Debra marvels at how the joy of the Lord fills her. She has experienced the miracle of what happens when we open ourselves up to allow God's love to move through us into someone else. I love this quote: "Every act of mercy done for someone who suffers is therefore also a direct kindness to Christ who dwells within that individual."[5]

If you want to see your loneliness, your longing for love, be filled, there is no more powerful way than to reach out and love someone else who is longing for it—whether you believe they deserve it or not. To Jesus this was such an important lesson that He chose to demonstrate it on His final night before His crucifixion.

Love in Action

Let's return again to where Jesus was celebrating Passover with His disciples in the upper room. He knew Judas would soon betray Him. The cross had cast a shadow even over Bethlehem—a shadow that had been with Him His whole life. And now it loomed close before Him. The disciples still did not comprehend it. They were just a bunch of "best buds" celebrating the feast together.

Then Jesus got up, laid aside His outer clothes, and put a towel around His waist. He poured water into a basin and began to wash the disciples' feet. Now, their feet were very dirty. Smelly. They wore sandals, and the roads were dusty and often covered with animal dung. The washing of feet was usually done by the servants of the home. This was not the role for Jesus! But He was kneeling, bent over their dirty feet, gently touching them, washing them, and wiping them with the towel He'd wrapped around His body. The towel got dirtier and dirtier as He went from one disciple to the next.

Then He got to Peter, who asked Him, "Lord, do You wash my feet?" Jesus answered, "What I do you do not realize now, but you will understand hereafter." Peter said to Him, "Never shall You wash my feet!" Jesus then said, "If I do not wash you, you have no part with Me" (John 13:6–8). Peter would have to surrender. Peter, being Peter, said, "Lord, then wash not only my feet, but also my hands and my head" (v. 9). He wanted all in. He was all or nothing. But Jesus calmly told him that was not what was called for.

I am sure they were all wondering what this was about. When Jesus finished and reclined back at the table, He asked them if they knew what He had done. He told them that they called Him "Teacher" and He was, but yet if He washed their feet as the teacher, they ought to be able to do the same for each other.

He let them know He was giving them an example to follow. He was illustrating what He'd told them: "Just as the Son of Man did not come to be served, but to serve, and to give His life a ransom for many" (Matt. 20:28).

The apostle Paul later said it this way:

Therefore if there is any encouragement in Christ, if there is any consolation of love, if there is any fellowship of the Spirit, if any affection and compassion, make my joy complete by being of the same mind, maintaining the same love, united in spirit, intent on one purpose. Do nothing from selfishness or empty conceit, but with humility of mind regard one another as more important than yourselves; do not merely look out for your own personal interests, but also for the interests of others. Have this attitude in yourselves which was also in Christ Jesus, who, although He existed in the form of God, did not regard equality with God a thing to be grasped, but emptied Himself, taking the form of a bond-servant and being made in the likeness of men. Being found in appearance as a man, He humbled Himself by becoming obedient to the point of death, even death on a cross. (Phil. 2:1–8)

Jesus had every right to demand others serve Him. He deserved it as no one ever had. But He chose to take on the role of a servant and serve those much lower than He.

If Jesus, as God of the universe, can take on the servant's role and do the dirty work, shouldn't we, too, serve each other? Maybe I should ask it like this: How do we serve each other in such a way?

It is amazing how helping others can lift your spirits, not to mention distract you from thinking about how miserable you are. This quote from licensed therapist Richard Hamon rings so true:

When we give of the heart we receive of the heart. The act of doing a good deed pushes out lonely feelings and opens the door to feeling more connected with others, and engenders a sense of belonging and attachment.[6]

Remember my mother's advice to me as a homesick girl at boarding school? It was, "Look around for someone who is more homesick than you, and go cheer them up." It is good advice for a homesick girl as well as anyone who feels lonely or is, in fact, alone.

There are many lonely people around you who need to be touched with love—perhaps not literally touched, but certainly figuratively. Just look. How many sit alone in church week after week? A simple introduction, a warm handshake of welcome, and an invitation to sit together could make a world of difference to that person.

As I write this during the 2020 COVID-19 shutdown, I have wondered how I can serve others in this time. I'm in an age group where I am more vulnerable and am urged to stay home. I feel sort of useless. I queried myself about it day after day. What could I do?

I took "goodies" down to the police station and firehouse. I figured they needed some support now more than ever. They are certainly on the front lines for our community and are often under attack. I just wanted to encourage them. I taught a twelve-week class of women prisoners in West Virginia during the pandemic. They obviously couldn't get out and I could not get in, so we did it via Zoom. I asked for their stories of loneliness and got touching letters from them. I also reached out to some men in a West Virginia prison—I'd attended their Bible college graduation last year. I asked them the same thing, to share their experiences of loneliness. I got letters from them that revealed heartache beyond what I could imagine. Broken lives. Broken families. Regrets. Rejection. Some had family so far from the prison that they didn't get any visits. They were lonely.

Prisoners are real people. People our society marginalizes and wants to forget. Jesus does not forget them, and He tells us to remember them. "For the LORD hears the needy and does not despise His who are prisoners" (Ps. 69:33).

These prisoners, most serving life sentences, have taken a four-year Bible college program to get their degrees. Then they are sent as missionaries to other prisons. This is a program started by Prison Seminaries Foundation headed by

Burl Cain, former warden of Angola Prison in Louisiana. He had a big vision, and these prisoners enjoy the benefits of it. The women in my class were taking part in a course to become mentors to others within their prison. I spent hours at my computer writing encouragement and Scriptures to all the prisoners who wrote to me.

I also get email through my website and I've tried to answer each one. I've had my new neighbors over for dinner— outside, on the screened-in porch. I came to realize that is a form of service during this time, and it not only serves others but keeps my mind off of myself. I think that is a key to dealing with loneliness.

My point is that the joy of service, of love in action, doesn't always need to be a huge life-altering event such as in Debra Moerke's case. Sometimes it's just a matter of being on the lookout for ways to touch people one at a time with an act of love. Richard Foster put it well: "There comes a new freedom to be with people. There is a new attentiveness to their needs, new responsiveness to their hurts."[7] These acts can be as simple as what I did on a recent Valentine's Day.

When you are alone, Valentine's Day is the pits! A couple of years ago, Valentine's Day was on a Friday. I was going to be home alone—and most likely feeling sorry for myself. I decided instead to have a dinner party for a number of my single lady friends. Some had been widowed during the last year, and I knew Valentine's Day would be a painful reminder of their loss. Others had been divorced for years and had no one to make them feel special. One was actually married, but her husband was traveling and I knew she would be lonely.

I had such fun thinking of ways to make this festive for them. I decorated. I made party favors. Everyone brought a dish to pass so each felt included. We went all out. We told each other about our best Valentine's Days and our worst. We laughed and had a grand time!

We began this chapter discussing touch, so it only seems fitting to end that way. Lissa has two stories that speak volumes about the power of reaching out to others in love when we are lonely. She wrote to me:

When I was newly divorced, women who had been my friends for years suddenly didn't seem to feel comfortable with me talking with their husbands at church. But two men told me they were making it their mission to give me a hug every Sunday (with their wives' permission, of course!). Those hugs helped me survive that awful time. I can't tell you how much they fed my soul and helped me go on.

I so understand Lissa's need and the gift those two couples gave to her. Our skin is the largest organ of our body. The sense of touch is one of our five senses. It is obviously important.

Countless times I've just wanted someone to wrap their arms around me and tell me it would be ok. I wanted a literal shoulder to cry on, a hand to hold. But that can get us into trouble too. It is vitally important that we keep any affection appropriate and safe. When that need feels too strong, look for an opportunity to hug your children or grandchildren, young or old, if you have been blessed to have them. Be very affectionate with them. On many significant occasions, my father held me in my adult years. He was very affectionate.

Lissa reminds us that God, who knows our secrets, is tenderly aware of our deepest needs. He also will use our acts of service to meet our own needs as well as the needs of others. She writes,

My heart hurt. It had been too long since I had someone hug me. Sure, there might be the brief, barely there hugs from friends along the way. Even those were sparse. The end of my marriage had left me more than financially destitute, as anyone who has been there can testify. The hole left by an absent partner is beyond comprehension. There is no more burrowing in for comfort, reassurance, or intimacy. And certainly, you can't just walk up to a friend and say, "Hey, how about a cuddle?"

I was in desperate need of being held. Of having some sort of close contact for more than a blink of an eye. I knew it was an impossibility, but still, that day I prayed, "Jesus, You know how much I hurt. You know my deepest desire. And You know what? This desire is no longer something I can ignore. It has become a desperate, crying need."

I prayed this as I gathered my things from my tiny thirteen-by-thirteen-foot garden cottage minihome. It was time for me to go help at the community center, a place where homeless and poor folks in our small city could get a hot meal and a word about Jesus. I helped there about four or five days a week, preparing and serving food, and hanging out with the guests and sharing their meal and stories with them. Once or twice a month, a small group from a local church would come to lend their hands in serving and provide the devotion for the evening.

That night, I arrived with my prayer still flowing through me. I helped fix the meal alongside the members of whatever small group had come to help. Not long before the devotion was to begin, a couple entered, the woman carrying a baby about five months old. She had been invited to sing as part of the pre-meal devotion. She looked around, a bit uncertain. Then she took one look at me and said, "Would you mind holding my baby while I sing?"

I gathered that baby in my arms. And because he fell asleep cuddled against my chest, he stayed there throughout dinner. It was all I could do not to weep. God had answered my prayer in a most unfathomable way. When I had prayed for this need to be met, I could never have conjured up this as the solution. I had felt my prayer was impossible to answer. Yet for our God, through whom nothing is impossible, I received an answer that allowed me to have not a brief hug, not even a lingering hug, but an hour-long snuggle with a precious, sweet smelling baby that fed my desperate need beyond what I could have imagined.

Jesus laid down His life for His friends—us. There is no greater love. His love is love in action. We, too, can love in action and service and touch. We all long to be loved, to have someone who will support and help us, to come to our rescue, to make our needs a priority, to touch us. Once we know and experience this with God, we can reach out to others in such a way that we express our love to them through love in action.

---------------------------------- **REACH** ----------------------------------

Once again, let's make each point a prayer.

R—Lord, I *recognize* that even though I now know You have seen me, You chose me, You know me, and I belong to You, I still feel that longing to be loved by You and by someone else.

E—Lord, today I *express* to You that I now am beginning to understand this verse from Matthew 7:12: "In everything, therefore, treat people the same way you want them to treat you." Lord, help me to do so with creativity and joy.

A—Lord, I *anticipate* that as I love others in action, I, too, will experience the power of being loved. Thank You in advance.

C—Lord, I am *connecting* to You right now. I love and adore You, my faithful God! Fill me with creative ideas on how to connect with others through acts of service from this day forward.

H—Father, I dedicate myself to loving others as You have loved me. In Jesus's name. Amen.

> **So then, while we have opportunity, let us do good to all people, and especially to those who are of the household of the faith.**
>
> Galatians 6:10

14

The Purpose and the Promise

Every human encounter can become a sacred conversation.

Trevor Hudson[1]

As I write these closing words, I am tucked away at a desk under the stairs of a friend's home. They have generously provided a quiet place for me to write. I am alone in my pursuit. Writing is a solitary activity—at least for me. (I know there are those who go to coffeehouses to write. Not me. I am far too distractible!) But as I am writing, I can hear my friend and her family in the living room playing games and chatting. To my surprise, it makes me feel just a little lonely. Because I live alone, it's rare for me to hear laughter and fun as I work at my computer, and now that I am hearing it, I feel drawn to set aside my writing and join them.

However, all I need to do is remind myself that I am alone for a reason right now. I believe that is key. We can endure loneliness far more effectively if we know it serves a purpose—and especially if we know it serves God's purposes.

Of course, pangs of loneliness sometimes sweep over me unexpectedly—perhaps when I see a couple walking hand in hand, or when I go to the doctor and there's nobody there to listen with me or be my advocate. Sometimes when I walk into church and have to decide if I want to sit alone or with someone else, it's an uncomfortable reminder that I'm by myself. We are human. Loneliness comes and goes with various circumstances. The difference for me, now that I've spent a year preparing for this book, is that I know what to do with that feeling. I can use my REACH exercise and anticipate how God is going to transform that fleeting sad emotion into an opportunity to connect more deeply with God and someone else. I actually have learned to see that loneliness is a gift.

Elisabeth Elliot offered great wisdom when she wrote of "seeing loneliness as a gift—to be received, and be offered back to God for His use."[2] I hope now that you've reached the final chapter you, too, might see loneliness as a gift, for as we've discussed, the pain of loneliness can awaken us to opportunities for transformation. Perhaps it is a call to choose the treasures of solitude and immerse yourself in some time with your Father where you might explore new depths of His love for you and His call on your life. Or maybe it will inspire you to reach out to connect to others and so enrich their lives as well as your own. Or it may reveal to you that you are longing to feel seen. It is a great reminder that God sees you just as you are and chooses to intervene in your life, and in turn, you could make someone's day by letting them know they are seen by you.

It's possible a pang of loneliness increases your longing for someone to choose you as special and want your company, and so reminds you that the God of the universe has chosen you for Himself and wants today as well as eternity with you. Or you may discover you long to feel truly known, or need reassurance that you belong or are deeply loved. Then what a gift it is! Because you'll be reminded to celebrate that God knows you intimately, that you belong to Him and His family, and that His love for you is immeasurable. Being reminded of those truths may just spur you on to reach out to others even in the smallest of ways, to demonstrate that you want to know them better, that you would enjoy being in community with them where you can share your gifts with one another, and above all that the God who dwells in you wants to reach out through you to love them. In every one of those scenarios, your loneliness is transformed into deepening your relationship with God and with others. Yes, loneliness is a gift.

But there is one additional purpose your loneliness might serve. To explore it, let's turn to a barren cell in a Roman prison in the ancient city of Philippi.

The Earthquake

When the jailer roughly shoved Paul and Silas into the windowless cell, more like a dungeon, the first thing they noticed was the stench. Then they saw the stocks. Clearly this was going to be a very unpleasant experience. After fastening both men's feet in the stocks, the jailer yanked on their chains to ensure they were securely locked. He wasn't taking any chances of escape. He'd been warned by the Roman magistrate to securely guard these two prisoners, which is why he'd locked them in one of the inner prison cells. Satisfied, he left them in silence.

Both men were bloodied and bruised by the severe beating they'd endured at the hands of the crowd. Paul broke the silence by praying for them both and offering thanks to God for protecting their lives, which inspired Silas to pray as well.

When they'd entered Philippi a few days before, they certainly hadn't expected to be arrested. They were passing through on their way to Antioch on an errand to deliver a letter from the church leaders in Jerusalem to the fledgling churches along the way. They'd had many opportunities to share the gospel as well, and the churches were being strengthened in their faith and increasing in numbers, so it had been an encouraging trip so far.

Once they were in Philippi a slave girl began following them around. She had a "spirit of divination" and so her owners profited greatly from her fortune-telling. For the past few days, she'd been their shadow, crying out, "These men are bond-servants of the Most High God, who are proclaiming to you the way of salvation" (Acts 16:17).

On this day, Paul turned to the young girl and commanded the spirit to come out of her. It did. But now she could no longer tell people their fortunes. Her owners, who had been using her, became livid when they realized their revenue stream had dried up. They grabbed Paul and Silas and put them in front of the local authorities, accusing them of throwing people into confusion. The authorities freaked out and ordered Paul and Silas to be beaten with rods. In a frenzy, the crowd inflicted many blows on the men. Now here they were in prison.

Did they moan and groan? Did they plot their escape? Were they mad at God for not protecting them? Did they throw a pity party? No! They started singing! Yes, singing. And being witnesses of the gospel to the other prisoners who were listening. This worship and songfest continued until midnight, when suddenly the earth began to violently shake. This earthquake was so great that the very foundations of the prison were shaken, and immediately every cell door broke open and everyone's chains fell off.

The jailer rushed to the prison, expecting to see all the prisoners gone, fearing that his head would roll. He was about to kill himself. That would be better than the horrible death the authorities would inflict on him and the disgrace his family would suffer.

> But Paul cried out with a loud voice, saying, "Do not harm yourself, for we are all here!" And he called for lights and rushed in, and trembling with fear he fell down before Paul and Silas, and after he brought them out, he said, "Sirs, what must I do to be saved?" (Acts 16:28–30)

They told him, "Believe in the Lord Jesus, and you will be saved, you and your household" (v. 31). The jailer was baptized, along with his household, and then he took Paul and Silas home, where he fed them and tended to their wounds.

I love that story on so many levels! I love God's dramatic rescue of Paul and Silas. I love the jailer going from nearly taking his own life to accepting the gift of eternal life along with his whole household. But what really speaks to me—and stirs me to greater faith—is that Paul and Silas, beaten, bruised, and bloodied, with their feet in stocks and an unknown future before them, were singing and praising God. They knew God had a plan and a purpose for them and could be trusted for the outcome, whatever that might be. They knew they were right in the center of that plan, and they knew Jesus was with them in it.

How did they know that? Because Jesus left no doubt in the minds and hearts of His disciples as to His purpose for them. After His resurrection He gave them a purpose and a promise. It is called the Great Commission, and it includes a promise that I believe has extra special meaning for those who are lonely:

> Go therefore and make disciples of all the nations, baptizing them in the name of the Father and the Son and the Holy Spirit, teaching them to observe all that I commanded you; and lo, *I am with you always*, even to the end of the age. (Matt. 28:19–20, emphasis added)

Mother Teresa understood the link between loneliness and spreading the gospel. She wrote,

> The greatest disease in the West today is not TB or leprosy; it is being unwanted, unloved, and uncared for. . . . The poverty in the West is a different kind of poverty—it is not only a poverty of loneliness but also of spirituality. There's a hunger for love, as there is a hunger for God.[3]

Loneliness reveals the hunger for God in the human heart. And who better than those who know God and also know the experience of loneliness to share the Good News of Jesus Christ with the lonely who don't yet know Him?

And as He has told us, He will be with us until the end of the age.

Releasing the Captives

> The Spirit of the LORD God is upon me,
> Because the Lord anointed me
> To bring good news to the afflicted;
> He has sent me to bind up the brokenhearted,
> To proclaim liberty to captives
> And freedom to prisoners. (Isa. 61:1)

Yes. He has sent us to the prisoners. And I believe that includes prisoners of loneliness. We've explored together that loneliness holds about half of our culture prisoner. And as we've discovered, the Lord can transform that loneliness into fellowship with Him and with others. Heaven is where God's desire for constant communion with His people—us—is finally completely satisfied and our desire to always be fully known and never alone is also wholly satisfied. In our loneliness, we can choose to reach out to others with the Good News of the gospel, helping others know an end to their loneliness as well.

As you and I take the risk to reach out to those who long to be seen, to be chosen, to be known, to belong, and to be loved, we know the One who can meet all those needs. Let's share that liberating news with them.

I understand something now that I didn't understand before doing the heart work of preparing for this book: *loneliness has little to do with the people—or lack of people—around you. It is a condition of the heart.* As you invite

God to transform your loneliness you are inviting Him to penetrate your heart and life more deeply. Now invite others to do the same.

I've been deeply blessed over the years through my involvement with prison ministry. In the previous chapter, I mentioned the amazing work of Burl Cain, former warden of the notorious Angola Prison in Louisiana. After my moving experience at Angola Prison, which I wrote about in my book *Forgiving My Father, Forgiving Myself: An Invitation to the Miracle of Forgiveness*, I stayed in contact with the folks there and soon became aware of Burl Cain's vision to put a seminary or Bible college in every prison he could through the work of Prison Seminaries Foundation. He believes in transformation, not reformation. And he believes that offering a prisoner the opportunity to be educated in God's Word is a way to give dignity and purpose to men and women who are serving long or lifetime sentences in our prisons. I became excited about his vision.

When I was able to attend a graduation of the Bible college in a prison in West Virginia, it was such an honor to be there. I was able to briefly meet with the men and pray with them before the ceremony. It was very emotional for me. They were all excited. The atmosphere was full of anticipation. I recognized some people from my previous visit to the prison. Like Antoine, who was now the pastor of the inmate prison chapel. He has a great smile and bright eyes.

One man spoke to me to tell me his son, whom he had not seen or heard from in fifteen years, was going to be there. He asked that I pray it would be a good reunion. He was anxious. I could only imagine.

The Bible college president was there, as were some of the professors—in full academic regalia—along with the glee club.

Fellow inmates were there, watching with interest. Many of them were enrolled in the program for the following semester.

"Pomp and Circumstance" began to play, and the capped and gowned men marched in, grinning from ear to ear while watching to catch a glimpse of their loved ones. This was a legitimate graduation. There was music and speeches. Even the governor was there to say how proud he was of them and how he supported this program.

The men's families were there for the most part—though some families had long since abandoned their sons. But the ones who came were eager to see their loved ones. The prison is tucked up in the mountains, way out of the way, but that didn't stop them. The mothers and grandmothers are the most faithful to come for visits. I watched their faces. The smiles. The tears. The pride. I could only contrast that in my heart with other times they had sat in support of their son, brother, uncle, such as in the courtroom, where they'd heard damning testimony as a horrible picture was painted of their family member. There was shame. So much shame. And then the sentence that sealed the deal.

And they came that day of graduation. Necks craning. Smiles that lit up the room. They were cautious and anxious. Now they would hear a different story than the one they'd experienced in the courtroom—and any tears would be those of joy.

When the final benediction was said, there was an eruption of applause.

Afterward, we were invited for a barbeque luncheon. The men fell on that immediately—it was definitely better than the regular fare at prison! There was cake and ice cream. Everyday things to me, but not to these men.

I stood and visited with all the graduates. I wanted to congratulate each one and meet their families. The man I'd spoken to beforehand about his son now told me he'd seen his son and was able to talk with him—reconciliation had begun! It made my heart sing. The whole day did.

But the program didn't end there. The graduates were then sent, two by two, to other prisons as missionaries. What a great concept! But this is a huge risk for a prisoner. They never know what they may be in for. I have heard from several who have been sent out. Adjusting to a new prison is not easy. But the gospel is being proclaimed and lives are being transformed. The men are excited about their new roles. Brad wrote me from his new prison to say, "I thank God I am here and that I am able to do the Lord's work in here . . . please keep me in prayer that I may be in step with the Spirit and walk worthy of the calling that God has placed before me."

As you can imagine, prison can be a desperately lonely place, and I've discussed loneliness with many of the prisoners I've met, men and women. This past spring, I invited one group of inmates to write to me about their loneliness experiences, and I received some moving letters. Then I opened a letter from Holly. It genuinely surprised me. With her permission, I'll share a portion of it with you.

You asked us to write about being lonely in prison but I honestly can't remember ever being lonely here. Incarceration has been the second-best thing of my life. [My] loneliness before incarceration was having a hole in your heart that nothing can fill, always searching for something that you can't find. So

*nothing in life can make you completely happy be-
cause of that void that can't be filled. . . . This loneliness leaves us a shadow of who we are, believing we
are nothing and nobody. . . .*

*I came to prison facing thirty years and thought it
would be the worst days of my life, but my Lord and
Savior changed that for me. Since giving my life to
Him while being incarcerated, it has been the very best
time of my life. He uses all things to the good of those
who love Him. And He will use my brokenness to His
glory.*

Holly may live behind bars, but she's living the freedom of
having God transform her loneliness. She attends Bible studies and is part of a Christian community where she knows
she belongs. She is part of a mentoring training program
as well, learning to share her faith with other prisoners.
When I picture Paul and Silas singing and praising God at
midnight in the prison, I easily picture Holly right there
with them. She understands her purpose and is living the
reality of Jesus's words, "I am with you always, even to the
end of the age" (Matt. 28:20).

I pray that you have now begun your own journey of
working with God to transform your loneliness into a deeper
connection with Him and with others, and I pray as well
that you will see the glorious privilege we have of sharing the
gospel with others who are lonely. What better news is there?

REACH

You will one day be in heaven and never feel lonely again. Until then, loneliness may come and go as your circumstances shift. That's perfectly normal. But when it comes, you don't want to camp there. Instead, you want to see your loneliness transformed!

For today's final REACH exercise, let's turn each of the REACH points into an "I will" statement you can revisit again and again to remind you of the choices you can make to work with God in transforming your loneliness into a deeper connection with God and others.

R—I will *recognize* my current loneliness can be transformed into a positive experience that accomplishes God's purposes and draws me into a closer relationship with Him and others.

E—I will *express* my desire for God to transform my loneliness into purpose—the purpose to share the good news of God's love with others so they may forever know they belong and are seen, chosen, known, and loved, now and for all eternity.

A—I will *anticipate* that God will use my loneliness to accomplish His purposes, especially the purpose to share my faith with others who are hungry for the good news that they can know Jesus personally.

C—I will *connect with God* by thanking Him that He sees me in my need, intervenes in my life, and assures me I am fully known and never alone. I will *connect with others* by sharing the good news that they are

248

seen, chosen, and known; belong to Him; and are loved immeasurably.

H—I will *honor* God in my loneliness by making my loneliness sacred—dedicating it to God to use me to draw others to Him.

Lo, I am with you always, even to the end of the age.

Matthew 28:20

Appendix A

The Most Important Friendship

God wants you in His family—it isn't complete without you. Isn't that a wonderful thought? You are wanted by the God of the universe. He loves you and wants you to be in His family, where you will belong to a great, worldwide, diverse community of those who believe in Jesus.

As I wrote in chapter 2, it is simply a matter of confessing your sin before Him and telling Him you believe Jesus died to cleanse and forgive you from those sins. Then ask Him to come in and take up residence in your heart and life.

You might pray a prayer like this:

God, I am lonely. I want to belong and be valued, but I have sinned and am unworthy. I am not good enough. So here today, I want to confess my sin to You. I believe Jesus died and rose again for me. Please forgive my sins and come live in my heart and life. I receive You as Lord and Savior. I give You my life. Help me to walk in this new life You have given me.

Thank You.

In Jesus's name. Amen.

If you prayed that prayer, you now belong to God's family. You have started a new life in Him. I am excited for you.

Let me give you a few suggestions that will help you grow in your relationship with God.

Tell someone about your decision—that helps to confirm your decision in your own mind.

Get a Bible, if you don't have one. And set aside a time each day to read and study it. The Gospel of John is a good place to begin. Ask God to help you understand what you are reading.

Pray every day. You don't need fancy words—just talk to Him as you would your best friend, because that is what He is. Tell God everything and ask for His help throughout the day.

Find a church that teaches what the Bible says and attend regularly. It is important to be around others who will encourage you in your faith. We need community. And a Bible-believing church is a great community of believers.

If you want to know more, I suggest going to the Billy Graham Evangelistic Association website and clicking on the tab "Grow in Your Faith" (https://billygraham.org/grow-your -faith/). You will find many resources and much encouragement there. There are even people standing by on a phone line you can talk to anytime, day or night.

Appendix B

The UCLA Loneliness Scale (Version 3)[1]

Instructions: Indicate how often each of the statements below is descriptive of you. (A note on scoring: in order to achieve an accurate score, the questions with an asterisk are "reverse scored." The numbers included in the chart reflect that.)

Statement	Never	Rarely	Sometimes	Often
*1. How often do you feel that you are "in tune" with the people around you?	4	3	2	1
2. How often do you feel that you lack companionship?	1	2	3	4
3. How often do you feel that there is no one you can turn to?	1	2	3	4
4. How often do you feel alone?	1	2	3	4
*5. How often do you feel part of a group of friends?	4	3	2	1
*6. How often do you feel that you have a lot in common with the people around you?	4	3	2	1

1. Daniel W. Russell, "UCLA Loneliness Scale (Version 3): Reliability, Validity, and Factor Structure," *Journal of Personality Assessment* 66:1 (February 1996): 20–40. Reprinted by permission of the publisher, Taylor & Francis Ltd, http://www.tandfonline.com.

Statement	Never	Rarely	Sometimes	Often
7. How often do you feel that you are no longer close to anyone?	1	2	3	4
8. How often do you feel that your interests and ideas are not shared by those around you?	1	2	3	4
*9. How often do you feel outgoing and friendly?	4	3	2	1
*10. How often do you feel close to people?	4	3	2	1
11. How often do you feel left out?	1	2	3	4
12. How often do you feel that your relationships with others are not meaningful?	1	2	3	4
13. How often do you feel that no one really knows you well?	1	2	3	4
14. How often do you feel isolated from others?	1	2	3	4
*15. How often do you feel you can find companionship when you want it?	4	3	2	1
*16. How often do you feel that there are people who really understand you?	4	3	2	1
17. How often do you feel shy?	1	2	3	4
18. How often do you feel that people are around you but not with you?	1	2	3	4
*19. How often do you feel that there are people you can talk to?	4	3	2	1
*20. How often do you feel that there are people you can turn to?	4	3	2	1
Score for each column:				
Total score:				

Total score less than 28 = No/Low Loneliness
Total score 28–43 = Moderate Loneliness
Total score greater than 43 = High Loneliness

Appendix C

Prayers and Verses for the Lonely

Prayers for Lonely Times

Jesus, I am alone. I feel all alone. I don't like that feeling. I see others together having a good time, and that makes me feel lonelier. I need Your help. Amen.

Almighty God, whose Son had nowhere to lay His head; grant that those who live alone may not be lonely in their solitude, but that, following in His steps, they may find fulfillment in loving You and their neighbors, through Jesus Christ our Lord. Amen.

Heavenly Father, the days of loneliness are long. The nights are even longer. I'm tired of it. Help me to feel Your presence. And please satisfy my longings with it. Sometimes I feel as if You are not enough. I am sorry for those feelings but I do feel them. Help me, please. Amen.

Heavenly Father, I know You are ever present with me. But I do not feel it right now. I feel all alone. I need a hug. I want a shoulder to cry on. What do I do in times like this?

I want to trust You. I want to believe You. I want to see You. I want to feel Your presence. Help me, Lord, to trust You anyway. Lord, I will trust You. And I will praise You in this time of aloneness. Amen.

Heavenly Father, I am tired of being alone. May I feel Your presence and know that I am really not alone. But if I don't, help me to trust You anyway and by faith, know You are with me. In Jesus's name. Amen.

Lord Jesus, You walked on earth as a human. You experienced all things as we do. So You must have been lonely at times. After all, You left heaven and came to earth as a baby. How foreign that must have been for You! So You do understand my feelings of loneliness. Thank you for understanding. Please Lord, now transform my loneliness to peace. Amen.

Lord, loneliness comes with a sense of weariness. I'm just tired of it all. Help me to raise my face to Your smile and be satisfied with You. You said You would "cause [Your] face to shine upon us" (Ps. 67:1). Please do it. Thank You for doing it in Jesus's name. Amen.

Heavenly Father, in these lonely hours give me a sense of gratitude for what You have done for me. Thank You for loving me. Help me to praise You for who You are.

You are enough to meet my every need as I trust You. In Jesus's name. Amen.

Heavenly Father, in these lonely times may I offer my loneliness as a praise to You. I don't want these to be wasted times but rather turn my heart toward You—as David did—and look for the needs of others who are lonely. Help me to reach beyond myself, quit thinking only about my loneliness, and see new opportunities to serve You. May You get the glory. In Jesus's name. Amen.

The Lord's Prayer from the *Book of Common Prayer*

Our Father which art in heaven, hallowed be Thy name.
Thy kingdom come, Thy will be done on earth as it is in heaven.
Give us this day our daily bread And forgive us our trespasses
as we forgive those who trespass against us.
And lead us not into temptation but deliver us from evil.
For Thine is the kingdom and the power and the glory forever.
Amen.

Thirty Scriptures for Lonely Times

Behold, I am with you and will keep you wherever you go, and will bring you back to this land; for I will not leave you until I have done what I have promised you.

Genesis 28:15

The LORD said, "I have surely seen the affliction of My people who are in Egypt, and have given heed to their cry because of their taskmasters, for I am aware of their sufferings. So

I have come down to deliver them from the power of the Egyptians, and to bring them up from that land to a good and spacious land, to a land flowing with milk and honey."

Exodus 3:7–8

And He said, "My presence shall go with you, and I will give you rest."

Exodus 33:14

The LORD bless you, and keep you;
The LORD make His face shine on you,
And be gracious to you;
The LORD lift up His countenance on you,
And give you peace.

Numbers 6:24–26

For He has not despised nor abhorred the affliction
   of the afflicted;
Nor has He hidden His face from him;
But when he cried to Him for help, He heard.

Psalm 22:24

The LORD is my shepherd,
I shall not want.
He makes me lie down in green pastures;
He leads me beside quiet waters.
He restores my soul;
He guides me in the paths of righteousness
For His name's sake.
Even though I walk through the valley of the shadow
   of death,
I fear no evil, for You are with me;

Your rod and Your staff, they comfort me.
You prepare a table before me in the presence of my
    enemies;
You have anointed my head with oil;
My cup overflows.
Surely goodness and lovingkindness will follow me
    all the days of my life,
And I will dwell in the house of the Lord forever.

Psalm 23

For my father and my mother have forsaken me,
But the Lord will take me up.

Psalm 27:10

I would have despaired unless I had believed that I
    would see the goodness of the Lord
In the land of the living.
Wait for the Lord;
Be strong and let your heart take courage;
Yes, wait for the Lord.

Psalm 27:13–14

You are my hiding place; You preserve me from
    trouble;
You surround me with songs of deliverance.

Psalm 32:7

The Lord of hosts is with us;
The God of Jacob is our stronghold.

Psalm 46:7

From the end of the earth I call to You when my
    heart is faint;
Lead me to the rock that is higher than I.

Psalm 61:2

A father of the fatherless and a judge for the
    widows,
Is God in His holy habitation.
God makes a home for the lonely;
He leads out the prisoners into prosperity,
Only the rebellious dwell in a parched land.

Psalm 68:5–6

I cry aloud with my voice to the LORD;
I make supplication with my voice to the LORD.
I pour out my complaint before Him;
I declare my trouble before Him.
When my spirit was overwhelmed within me,
You knew my path.
In the way where I walk
They have hidden a trap for me.
Look to the right and see;
For there is no one who regards me;
There is no escape for me;
No one cares for my soul.
I cried out to You, O LORD;
I said, "You are my refuge,
My portion in the land of the living.
"Give heed to my cry,
For I am brought very low;
Deliver me from my persecutors,
For they are too strong for me.
"Bring my soul out of prison,

So that I may give thanks to Your name;
The righteous will surround me,
For You will deal bountifully with me."

Psalm 142:1–7

I was asleep but my heart was awake.
A voice! My beloved was knocking:
"Open to me, my sister, my darling,
My dove, my perfect one!
For my head is drenched with dew,
My locks with the damp of the night."

Song of Solomon 5:2

Do not fear, for I am with you;
Do not anxiously look about you, for I am your God.
I will strengthen you, surely I will help you,
Surely I will uphold you with My righteous right
    hand.

Isaiah 41:10

I will lead the blind by a way they do not know,
In paths they do not know I will guide them.
I will make darkness into light before them
And rugged places into plains.
These are the things I will do,
And I will not leave them undone.

Isaiah 42:16

The LORD's lovingkindnesses indeed never cease,
For His compassions never fail
They are new every morning;

Great is Your faithfulness.

Lamentations 3:22–23

Though the fig tree should not blossom
And there be no fruit on the vines,
Though the yield of the olive should fail
And the fields produce no food,
Though the flock should be cut off from the fold
And there be no cattle in the stalls,
Yet I will exult in the LORD,
I will rejoice in the God of my salvation.

Habakkuk 3:17–18

Are not two sparrows sold for a cent? And yet not one of them will fall to the ground apart from your Father. But the very hairs of your head are all numbered.

Matthew 10:28–30

And He said to them, "Come away by yourselves to a secluded place and rest a while." (For there were many people coming and going, and they did not even have time to eat.) They went away in the boat to a secluded place by themselves.

Mark 6:31–32

While they were telling these things, He Himself stood in their midst and said to them, "Peace be to you."

Luke 24:36

Do not let your heart be troubled; believe in God, believe also in Me. In My Father's house are many dwelling places; if it were not so, I would have told you; for I go to prepare a place for you. If I go and prepare a place for you, I will come again and receive you to Myself, that where I am, there you may be also.

John 14:1–3

I will ask the Father, and He will give you another Helper, that He may be with you forever.

John 14:16

No longer do I call you slaves, for the slave does not know what his master is doing; but I have called you friends, for all things that I have heard from My Father I have made known to you. You did not choose Me but I chose you, and appointed you that you would go and bear fruit, and that your fruit would remain, so that whatever you ask of the Father in My name He may give to you.

John 15:15–16

The Spirit Himself testifies with our spirit that we are children of God, and if children, heirs also, heirs of God and fellow heirs with Christ, if indeed we suffer with Him so that we may also be glorified with Him.

Romans 8:16–17

Now may the God of hope fill you with all joy and peace in believing, so that you will abound in hope by the power of the Holy Spirit.

Romans 15:13

Draw near to God and He will draw near to you. Cleanse your hands, you sinners; and purify your hearts, you double-minded.

James 4:8

I can do all things through Him who strengthens me.

Philippians 4:13

At my first defense no one supported me, but all deserted me; may it not be counted against them. But the Lord stood with me and strengthened me.

2 Timothy 4:16–17

I will never desert you, nor will I ever forsake you.

Hebrews 13:5

Psalms for Meditation in Lonely Times

Psalm 69	Psalm 91
Psalm 88	Psalm 139

Appendix D

Reader's Discussion Guide

Chapter 1: The Pelican in the Wilderness

1. What does loneliness feel like to you? Describe it.
2. Would you describe a lonely time in your life?
3. Discuss the statement, "For loneliness, unchallenged, has the power to eat away at our emotional, spiritual, and physical health." Have you seen this dynamic play out in someone's life? Your own life?
4. Do you believe there is a stigma to loneliness? What is it? Why is it?
5. How do you relate to King David's pelican?

Chapter 2: The One Who Sees

1. What comforts you when you feel lonely?
2. Where have you come from? And where are you going?
3. If you were Hagar, how would you have felt about going back to Sarai's tent?

4. How are you investing yourself in God's plan for you?

5. Share a story of being lost. How did you feel? How is being lonely like being lost?

Chapter 3: The Best of Company

1. What did you think of the idea that God is in community? What aspect of God desiring community speaks to you?

2. What new thing or things did you learn about God?

3. Why do you think Jesus chose community here on earth? How might that alter your thoughts on community?

4. How can you build community into your life?

5. Who is your community you turn to?

6. How does your community spur you on to deeper growth?

7. What variations of community do you have in your life?

8. Tell the story of how and when you made Jesus your personal Lord and Savior.

Chapter 4: The Well-Kept Secret

1. Which statistic about loneliness surprised you most? Comforted you most? Challenged you most?

2. Share what you learned about yourself when you answered the twenty questions in appendix B.

3. React to this statement from Brené Brown: "The way we engage with social media is like fire—you can use them to keep yourself warm and nourished, or you

can burn down the barn." How do you use social media?

4. Which of the four reasons for increased loneliness is the most significant in your life?

Chapter 5: The Dark Side of Loneliness

1. Have you ever run from God and found yourself lonely? Can you share that story?

2. Describe the qualities you believe are necessary in a trusted confidant. Which of those qualities do you have yourself?

3. As you read about the physical toll of loneliness, what surprised you?

4. How are you intentional about social interactions?

5. If you are suffering in some way, see if you can trace the root to loneliness. If so, what are some steps you can take to begin to work on it?

Chapter 6: The Transformation of Loneliness

1. What characteristics about Ruth's mother stood out to you?

2. Discuss the statement, "Loneliness, you see, can be a gift. The pain of loneliness is a powerful motivator." How can it be so for you?

3. How can your loneliness be transformed into persistence like Noah?

4. How can you display trust in God in your loneliness? What would it look like?

5. Discuss God's answer to Job. Would you have found it satisfactory? Explain.

6. What does it mean to partner with God in your transformation?

Chapter 7: The Treasures of Solitude

1. What do you think about this statement: "Loneliness can . . . give a person less self-control over behaviors, cravings, and emotions and therefore make them more susceptible to addictive behaviors"? How have you seen that play out in your life or a loved one's life?

2. Which step in REACH is the most difficult for you? Why? Which is the most powerful? Why?

3. What do you think about the concept of making your loneliness "sacred"? How might you achieve that?

4. Who can you connect with this week?

Chapter 8: The Cultivation of Solitude

1. In what ways can we transform loneliness into solitude?

2. Can you share an experience where anticipated loneliness was transformed?

3. How do you create solitude?

4. Could you add to the five benefits of solitude?

5. What impressed you about King David? About the shepherd?

Chapter 9: The Choice to REACH

1. Share an experience where you felt utterly alone and yet God's presence was very real to you.

2. What crowds in your life prevent you from solitude?

3. How can you cultivate solitude with God today in your life?

4. When is a good time for you to get alone with God?

5. Can you share a time when you prayed earnestly and God ministered to you?

6. What are the best ways you can create a dedicated time to slip away with God?

Chapter 10: The Affirmation of Being Chosen

1. What do you think about the chat bench idea? Would you ever sit on one and chat? Why or why not?

2. When have you ever felt invisible?

3. Discuss this statement by Melissa Febos: "There are few experiences as powerful as articulating your vulnerability in the presence of another." Have you ever done that? Can you share what it felt like?

4. Why do you think it is so hard to break into a new community or church, like Brittany discovered?

5. As you meditated on Psalm 139, what did you discover?

6. If you were Thomas, how would you have felt seeing Jesus in front of you and inviting you to touch His wounds, knowing He knew your unbelief?

7. Do you believe vulnerability is courageous or weak? How do you respond when someone is vulnerable with you?

8. What was a new insight into John the Baptist? How can you apply that to your life?

Chapter 11: The Comfort of Being Known

1. When have you ever felt different or left out?
2. What do you think about Jesus seeing you and knowing your name? How does that impact your life?
3. How has friendship with God transformed you? How might it?
4. Think about being chosen by God. How does that impact you? What do you feel?
5. Discuss this statement: "In calling you to love others Jesus is trusting you to feed and nourish and bless others, and that will create the kind of connection to others that satisfies loneliness."
6. In what way can you love, nourish, and bless someone today?
7. How can you simply reach out to someone this week?
8. Of the five REACH steps at the end of this chapter, which one will you tackle?

   • How can you recognize your own loneliness?
   • Will you make a plan to talk to God and one other person about it?
   • What do you anticipate God will do to transform it?
   • How will you connect with God and who will you reach out to?

Chapter 12: The Security of Belonging

1. What is unique about you in your family?
2. What goes through your mind and heart when you consider the idea of God as "Daddy"?

3. Talk about a group or community where you feel
   you belong. If you don't have one, what would be
   the kind of group where you would get that sense of
   belonging?
4. What would make you feel more connected to God?
5. Choose a verse to trigger your awareness that God is
   your "Abba" and you belong to Him. Consider memorizing it.
6. How do you cultivate your relationship with God?
7. If you have ever kept a "gratitude journal," share
   how that affected your outlook.
8. How can you intentionally reach out to someone in
   the next week?
9. What is your gift you can employ to build up Christ's
   body?
10. Discuss Cynthia's statement: "Be the community
    you wish you had, and you'll eventually find yourself
    surrounded by people." How can you start to be the
    community you wish you had?

Chapter 13: The Assurance of Being Loved

1. Had you been the leper, would you have risked going
   to Jesus? Why or why not?
2. What are the risks of striving to love as Jesus does?
3. What would you have done had you been in Debra
   Moerke's place? How would you have responded to
   Karen's request for a visit?
4. I hope you noticed the interesting statement that, as
   Jesus was washing the disciples' feet, "the towel got
   dirtier and dirtier as He went from one disciple to

the next." What significance do you think the dirty towel has as we think of serving others?

5. In what ways are you serving others in your church, community, and family?

6. What are some reasons people are reluctant to serve the needs of others?

7. In what way has God met your need for touch?

Chapter 14: The Purpose and the Promise

1. What do you think of Elisabeth Elliot's quote, "seeing loneliness as a gift—to be received, and be offered back to God for His use"?

2. If you had been beaten and locked down in stocks in a dungeon, how would you react?

3. What is God's purpose for your loneliness? If you do not know it, will you pray and ask Him to show it to you?

4. Consider who you know who might be lonely. How can you reach out to them in the coming weeks?

5. How can you share the Good News with someone who is lonely? (A good way to begin is to give them this book!)

6. In what ways do you now see your loneliness as a gift?

Acknowledgments

Turning in a manuscript is just the first step in a long process. There are many people involved in the creation of a book. It is never just one person or even two. It's a whole team. And I am blessed with a great team.

This book is as much Cindy Lambert's as it is mine. She and I have worked together for almost twenty years. She has been more than an editor and collaborative writer. She is my friend. We speak the same heart language.

It was Cindy who suggested I work on a book on loneliness, and she also suggested we have research done for this book. She tackled it, made sense of it, and made it readable. And it gives real depth to this book.

Cindy is a master at her craft. There is none better. I gave her all sorts of odd pieces—she must have felt buried—and she was able from that to see the big picture and get the little pieces organized. She always kept her focus on the big picture and then told me what I had to do to fill in the blanks.

I am forever grateful for her professionalism, her kindness, her sense of humor, and her sweet spirit.

And I am grateful for her understanding and gentle husband, Dave. A true prince among men! He doesn't fuss as she crawls out of bed at two a.m. to work on a chapter. (Or maybe he does!)

To my faithful and kind agent, Wes Yoder: without you I would never have been able to join the Baker Publishing family, which is one I have come to love and appreciate. Ambassador Speakers Bureau and Literary Agency truly is a family business. To my Baker editor extraordinaire, Rebekah Guzman: your enthusiastic response to our manuscript was overwhelming. To Lindsey Spoolstra, Rachel O'Connor, Brianna DeWitt, and the whole team at Baker: you give your all to excellence, and I so appreciate it. And Lissa Halls Johnson, my freelance editor: you have an eagle eye and made sure we got it right. Your details were spot-on.

I am grateful for my ministry prayer team, who are so faithful to pray. We gather together once a month at Len and Kathy Hassell's home in Charlottesville. They've prayed us over the humps and cheered me on.

And thanks to my friends Peggy Garvey, who makes sure I get out and have some fun, and Tamey Meyer, who keeps my house in order. And Michelle Fitzgerald: you can do just about anything—you are so organized and efficient. And Lindsay and Wayne Williams, thanks for knocking the kinks out of my body from sitting too long!

I am grateful for my new church, Tabernacle Presbyterian. I've had a hard time getting to know the folks behind their masks, but little by little! I am enjoying the good teaching and being challenged in my walk with the Lord.

I have a host of cheerleaders who encourage me on to thank as well. My sister friend, Cindy McCrory. We talk most afternoons. And during COVID I have had the joy of a conference call three times a week with great friends—two in Georgia and two in a nearby city. We discuss the issues of the day. We share one another's burdens. They have encouraged me and prayed for me regularly. And my Texas friend, Irby Bair, who really believes in what I do and appreciates my writing. Everyone needs an Irby in their lives!

My precious friend Martha Ayers is a mentor, friend, godly example, and second mother. She has prayed for me through the years, faithfully and lovingly. She was eager to go on to heaven and just after Christmas 2020 went to meet her Savior face-to-face. She is now seeing Him in His glory. I will miss her beyond expression.

Once again, this book began to be written in the Cayman Islands at the home of Russ and Mary Brandes. No more generous people are there. And thanks to Nancy and Al Oyer, who brought the video series *Poldark* so we could all watch it together, even as COVID-19 was descending on the world.

And always, I am grateful for my children and grandchildren, who delight my heart and keep me from getting too lonely. I love it when my grandson comes to my door when he is walking their black Lab, or my granddaughters run in to borrow something from "Mackie's grocery" because their mother doesn't have any or has run out of it. We all have Sunday lunch together each week. I am so proud of each one. And so blessed.

Notes

Chapter 1 The Pelican in the Wilderness

1. Trevor Hudson, *Beyond Loneliness* (Nashville: Upper Room Books, 2016), 22.
2. Vivek Murthy, "Connecting at Work," *Harvard Business Review: The Big Idea* (September 2017), https://hsc.unm.edu/school -of-medicine/education/assets/doc/wellness/murthy-loneliness .pdf.
3. Murthy, "Connecting at Work."
4. Jacqueline Olds and Richard S. Schwartz, *The Lonely American* (Boston: Beacon, 2010), 9.
5. Guy Winch, "10 Surprising Facts about Loneliness," *Psychology Today*, October 21, 2014, https://www.psychologytoday .com/us/blog/the-squeaky-wheel/201410/10-surprising-facts-about -loneliness.
6. Neil Howe, "Millennials and the Loneliness Epidemic," *Forbes*, May 3, 2019, https://www.forbes.com/sites/neilhowe/2019 /05/03/millennials-and-the-loneliness-epidemic/#37e8fc30767.

Chapter 2 The One Who Sees

1. Annie Lent, "For the Lonely," *Life: Beautiful* (Summer 2019), 54.
2. Hudson, *Beyond Loneliness*, 114.
3. Elisabeth Elliot, *Loneliness: It Can Be a Wilderness. It Can Be a Pathway to God* (Nashville: Nelson, 1988), 22.

Chapter 3 The Best of Company

1. Hudson, *Beyond Loneliness*, 37.
2. Lent, "For the Lonely," 52.

Chapter 4 The Well-Kept Secret

1. Brené Brown, *Braving the Wilderness* (New York: Random House, 2014), 55.
2. Kasley Killam, "In the Midst of the Pandemic, Loneliness Has Leveled Out," *Scientific American*, August 18, 2020, https://www.scientificamerican.com/article/in-the-midst-of-the-pandemic-loneliness-has-leveled-out/.
3. Killam, "In the Midst of the Pandemic."
4. Howe, "Millennials and the Loneliness Epidemic."
5. Rhitu Chatterjee, "Americans Are a Lonely Lot, and Young People Bear the Heaviest Burden," *NPR*, May 1, 2018, https://www.npr.org/sections/health-shots/2018/05/01/606588504/americans-are-a-lonely-lot-and-young-people-bear-the-heaviest-burden.
6. CBS News, "Many Americans Are Lonely, and Gen Z Most of All, Study Finds," *CBS News*, May 3, 2018, https://www.cbsnews.com/news/many-americans-are-lonely-and-gen-z-most-of-all-study-finds/.
7. Amy Novotney, "The Risks of Social Isolation," *Monitor on Psychology* 50, no. 5 (May 2019): 32, https://www.apa.org/monitor/2019/05/ce-corner-isolation.
8. CBS News, "Many Americans Are Lonely."
9. Brian Resnick, "22 Percent of Millennials Say They Have 'No Friends,'" *Vox*, August 1, 2019, https://www.vox.com/science-and-health/2019/8/1/20750047/millennials-poll-loneliness.
10. Resnick, "22 Percent of Millennials."
11. Jamie Ballard, "Millennials Are the Loneliest Generation," YouGov, July 30, 2019, https://today.yougov.com/topics/lifestyle/articles-reports/2019/07/30/loneliness-friendship-new-friends-poll-survey.
12. Ballard, "Millennials Are the Loneliest Generation."
13. Resnick, "22 Percent of Millennials."
14. Ballard, "Millennials Are the Loneliest Generation."
15. Frank J. Ninivaggi, "Loneliness: A New Epidemic in the USA," *Psychology Today*, February 12, 2019, https://www.psychologytoday.com/us/blog/envy/201902/loneliness-new-epidemic-in-the-usa.
16. Francie Hart Broghammer, "Death by Loneliness," *RealClear Policy*, May 6, 2019, https://www.realclearpolicy.com/articles/2019/05/06/death_by_loneliness_111185.html.
17. Dennis Prager, "Why Are So Many Young People Unhappy?," *Prager's Column*, January 21, 2020, https://www.dennisprager.com/why-are-so-many-young-people-unhappy/.

18. Howe, "Millennials and the Loneliness Epidemic."

19. Howe, "Millennials and the Loneliness Epidemic."

20. Howe, "Millennials and the Loneliness Epidemic."

21. Broghammer, "Death by Loneliness."

22. American Osteopathic Association, "Survey Finds Nearly Three-Quarters (72 Percent) of Americans Feel Lonely," The Harris Poll, accessed January 25, 2021, https://theharrispoll.com/a-new-survey-of-more-than-2000-american-adults-found-72-percent-report-having-felt-a-sense-of-loneliness-with-nearly-a-third-31-percent-experiencing-loneliness-at-least-once-a-week-the-survey-was/.

23. Calypso, "How Technology Is Increasing Loneliness in America," *Medium*, December 7, 2017, https://medium.com/@melissalovestowrite/how-technology-is-increasing-loneliness-in-america-c6dbdbab8f5b.

24. Luke Fernandez and Susan J. Matt, "Americans Were Lonely Long before Technology," *Slate*, June 19, 2019, https://slate.com/technology/2019/06/bored-lonely-angry-stupid-excerpt-technology-loneliness-history.html.

25. Chatterjee, "Americans Are a Lonely Lot."

26. Chatterjee, "Americans Are a Lonely Lot."

27. Brown, *Braving the Wilderness*, 140.

28. Sherry Amatenstein, "Not So Social Media: How Social Media Increases Loneliness," *PsyCom*, November 15, 2019, https://www.psycom.net/how-social-media-increases-loneliness/; Terry Brown, "Does Technology Make Us More Alone?," *IT Chronicles*, August 6, 2019, https://itchronicles.com/technology/does-technology-make-us-more-alone/.

29. Howe, "Millennials and the Loneliness Epidemic."

30. Julianne Holt-Lunstad, "The Potential Public Health Relevance of Social Isolation and Loneliness: Prevalence, Epidemiology, and Risk Factors," *Public Policy and Aging Report* 27, no. 4 (2017): 127–30, https://academic.oup.com/ppar/article/27/4/127/4782506.

31. American Psychological Association, "'Loneliness Epidemic' May Be Due to Increasing Aging Population," *ScienceDaily*, December 10, 2019, https://www.sciencedaily.com/releases/2019/12/191210111711.htm.

32. American Osteopathic Association, "Survey Finds Nearly Three-Quarters."

33. Novotney, "The Risks of Social Isolation."

34. Broghammer, "Death by Loneliness."

35. R. Albert Mohler Jr., "The Briefing: Friday, April 24, 2020," *Albert Mohler*, April 24, 2020, https://albertmohler.com/2020/04/24/briefing-4-24-20.

36. Harmeet Kaur, "The Coronavirus Pandemic Is Making Earth Vibrate Less," *CNN*, April 3, 2020, https://www.cnn.com/2020/04/02/world/coronavirus-earth-seismic-noise-scn-trnd/index.html.

37. Novotney, "The Risks of Social Isolation." See also Julianne Holt-Lunstad et al., "Loneliness and Social Isolation as Risk Factors for Mortality: A Meta-Analytic Review," *Perspectives on Psychological Science* 10, no. 2 (2015), https://scholarsarchive.byu.edu/cgi/viewcontent.cgi?article=3024&context=facpub.

38. Broghammer, "Death by Loneliness."

39. Richard Cimino, "The Millennials' Loneliness Gap and the Religion Factor," *Ahead of the Trend*, October 21, 2019, http://blogs.thearda.com/trend/featured/the-millennials-loneliness-gap-and-the-religion-factor/.

40. Cimino, "The Millennials' Loneliness Gap."

41. Prager, "Why Are So Many Young People Unhappy?"

42. Broghammer, "Death by Loneliness."

Chapter 5 The Dark Side of Loneliness

1. John T. Cacioppo and William Patrick, *Loneliness* (New York: W. W. Norton, 2008), 34.

2. Ruth Graham, *In Every Pew Sits a Broken Heart* (Grand Rapids: Zondervan, 2004), 103.

3. Broghammer, "Death by Loneliness."

4. Novotney, "The Risks of Social Isolation."

5. RainbowKids, "Failure to Thrive," RainbowKids.com, accessed January 25, 2021, https://www.rainbowkids.com/special-needs/developmental-needs/failure-to-thrive.

6. Murthy, "Connecting at Work." https://hsc.unm.edu/school-of-medicine/education/assets/doc/wellness/murthy-loneliness.pdf.

7. Murthy, "Connecting at Work."

8. Howe, "Millennials and the Loneliness Epidemic."

9. Harrison Wein, ed., "Care and Connection: Loneliness Affects All Ages," *News in Health*, August 2018, https://newsinhealth.nih.gov/2018/08/care-connection.

10. Winch, "10 Surprising Facts about Loneliness."

11. Novotney, "The Risks of Social Isolation."

12. Resnick, "22 Percent of Millennials."

Chapter 6 The Transformation of Loneliness

1. Elisabeth Elliot, *The Path of Loneliness* (Grand Rapids: Revell, 2007), 89.

2. "Transformation," Google dictionary search, accessed January 19, 2021, https://www.google.com/search?q=Transformation&oq=Transformation&aqs=chrome..69i57j0i433j46i175i199i433j0i433l2j46i175i199j0i433l2.2532j1j7&sourceid=chrome&ie=UTF-8.

3. Elliot, *Path of Loneliness*, 127.

4. "Read More about Jane Merchant," *Tennessee4me*, accessed January 25, 2021, http://www.tn4me.org/sapage.cfm/sa_id/252/era_id/8/major_id/12/minor_id/33.

5. Ruth Bell Graham, *Sitting by My Laughing Fire* (Nashville: Word Books, 1977), from the explanation.

6. "Gretchen Rubin Quotes," BrainyQuote, accessed February 22, 2021, https://www.brainyquote.com/quotes/gretchen_rubin_619371.

7. Hudson, *Beyond Loneliness*, 60.

Chapter 7 The Treasures of Solitude

1. "Paul Tillich Quotes," Goodreads, accessed February 22, 2021, https://www.goodreads.com/quotes/218726-language-has-created-the-word-loneliness-to-express-the-pain.

2. Emily S. Elliott, "Thou Didst Leave Thy Throne" (1864), public domain, https://hymnary.org/text/thou_didst_leave_thy_throne_and_thy_king.

3. Hara Estroff Marano, "What Is Solitude?," *Psychology Today*, July 1, 2003, https://www.psychologytoday.com/us/articles/200307/what-is-solitude.

4. Marano, "What Is Solitude?"

5. Elliot, *Loneliness*, 127.

6. Dean Griffiths, "What's the Difference between Solitude and Loneliness?," *Psychreg*, December 13, 2017, https://www.psychreg.org/difference-between-solitude-and-loneliness/.

7. Fernandez and Matt, "Americans Were Lonely."

8. Anne-Laure Le Cunff, "Loneliness or Solitude: The Case for Being Alone," *Ness Labs*, accessed January 25, 2021, https://nesslabs.com/loneliness-solitude.

9. Tokunboh Adeyemo, ed., *Africa Bible Commentary* (Grand Rapids: Zondervan, 2006), 605.

10. Lydia Brownback, *Finding God in My Loneliness* (Wheaton: Crossway, 2017), 67.

11. Richard Foster, *Celebration of Discipline* (New York: Harper & Row, 1978), 86.

Chapter 8 The Cultivation of Solitude

1. Henri Nouwen, *The Way of the Heart: The Spirituality of the Desert Fathers and Mothers*, rev. ed. (New York: Harper Collins, 1991), 18.

2. H. D. Spence and Joseph S. Exell, *The Pulpit Commentary* vol. 16 (Grand Rapids: Eerdmans, 1961), 225.

3. Elaine K. Luo, "Hematidrosis: Is Sweating Blood Real?," *Healthline*, March 14, 2017, https://www.healthline.com/health/hematidrosis#causes.

4. Nouwen, *Way of the Heart*, 18.

5. Nouwen, *Way of the Heart*, 30.

Chapter 9 The Choice to REACH

1. "Viktor E. Frankl Quotes," Goodreads, accessed February 22, 2021, https://www.goodreads.com/quotes/51356-everything-can-be-taken-from-a-man-but-one-thing.

2. "The Connection between Loneliness & Substance Abuse," Lasting Recovery, accessed January 25, 2021, https://lastingrecovery.com/the-connection-between-loneliness-and-substance-abuse/.

3. Johann Hari, "Everything You Think You Know about Addiction Is Wrong," TED Talk, July 9, 2015, https://www.youtube.com/watch?v=PY9DcIMGxMs.

4. Vertava Health, "Addiction, Isolation and the Cycle of Loneliness," *Vertava Health*, accessed January 25, 2021, https://www.addictioncampuses.com/blog/addiction-isolation-and-the-cycle-of-loneliness/.

Chapter 10 The Affirmation of Being Chosen

1. Emilie Griffen, *Green Leaves for Later Years* (Downers Grove, IL: InterVarsity, 2012), 78.

2. Hudson, *Beyond Loneliness*, 22.

3. Hudson, *Beyond Loneliness*, 95.

4. Mother Teresa, *A Simple Path* (New York: Ballantine Books, 1995), 79.

5. Health Resources and Services Administration, "The 'Loneliness Epidemic,'" *HRSA*, accessed January 25, 2021, https://www.hrsa.gov/enews/past-issues/2019/january-17/loneliness-epidemic.

Chapter 11 The Comfort of Being Known

1. Brown, *Braving the Wilderness*, 144–45.
2. Adapted from Matt Lloyd, "'Happy to Chat' Benches: The Woman Getting Strangers to Talk," *BBC News*, October 18, 2019, https://www.bbc.com/news/uk-wales-50000204. If you want to get some ideas to create your own chat bench, check out http://www.sclt.us/chat-bench/4594670652.
3. Melissa Febos, "Can You Hear Me Now?," *O Magazine* (November 2019), 128.
4. Brown, *Braving the Wilderness*, 154.

Chapter 12 The Security of Belonging

1. Hudson, *Beyond Loneliness*, 41.
2. Wein, "Care and Connection."
3. Pam Rhodes, "Foreword," in Jennifer Page, *Freedom from Loneliness: 52 Ways to Stop Feeling Lonely* (CreateSpace, 2012).
4. Cacioppo and Patrick, *Loneliness*, 19.
5. Deborah Gyapong, "Religion Has Role in Fighting Loneliness," *Catholic Register*, July 12, 2019, https://www.catholicregister.org/item/29892-religion-has-role-in-fighting-loneliness.
6. John Piper, "We Need Each Other: Christian Fellowship as a Means of Perseverance," *Desiring God*, April 19, 2017, https://www.desiringgod.org/messages/we-need-each-other.
7. Lent, "For the Lonely," 53.
8. Novotney, "The Risks of Social Isolation."
9. Broghammer, "Death by Loneliness."

Chapter 13 The Assurance of Being Loved

1. Elliot, *Loneliness*, 144.
2. Debra Moerke with Cindy Lambert, *Murder, Motherhood, and Miraculous Grace* (Carol Stream, IL: Tyndale, 2019), 104–5.
3. Moerke with Lambert, *Murder, Motherhood, and Miraculous Grace*, 107.

4. Moerke with Lambert, *Murder, Motherhood, and Miraculous Grace*, 107–8.

5. Hudson, *Beyond Loneliness*, 79.

6. Richard Hamon, "How to Cure Loneliness: Simple, Effective Steps You Can Take Right Now," *Happy Relationships*, accessed January 25, 2021, https://www.happy-relationships.com /cureloneliness.html.

7. Foster, *Celebration of Discipline*, 95.

Chapter 14 The Purpose and the Promise

1. Hudson, *Beyond Loneliness*, 66.

2. Elliot, *Loneliness*, 147.

3. Mother Teresa, *Simple Path*, 79.

Discover the
TRANSFORMATIVE POWER
of Forgiveness

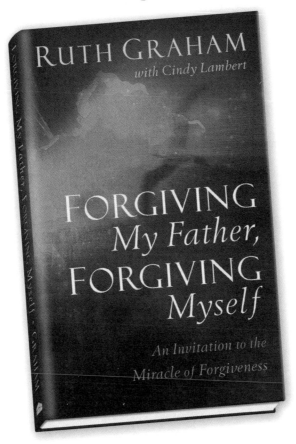

"Through her most vulnerable writing, Ruth Graham shares with us the topic of forgiveness. In this encouraging book, she incorporates her own personal experiences as well as biblical Scripture to help guide us as readers to a better understanding of what forgiveness means and why we should choose forgiveness."

—**Mark Batterson,** *New York Times* bestselling author of *The Circle Maker* and lead pastor of National Community Church

BakerBooks
a division of Baker Publishing Group
www.BakerBooks.com

Available wherever books and ebooks are sold.

Ruth Graham
MINISTRIES

Ruth Graham Ministries seeks to motivate people by God's grace and unconditional love from a place of woundedness to a place of wholeness in Christ. Ruth Graham Ministries seeks to create safe places where people can begin their journey to wholeness in Christ.

WWW.RUTHGRAHAM.COM

Ruth Graham is represented by Ambassador Literary Agency
Nashville, Tennessee

TO SCHEDULE RUTH TO SPEAK FOR YOUR EVENT,
PLEASE CONTACT: info@AmbassadorAgency.com

 Ruth Graham    @RuthBellGraham

Connect with

Relevant. Intelligent. Engaging.

Sign up for announcements about new and upcoming titles at

BakerBooks.com/SignUp

@ReadBakerBooks